HOPE
IN
HER

Hope in Her

ISBN (paperback): 979-8-9865862-8-1
ISBN (hardback): 979-8-9865862-9-8
ISBN (ebook): 978-1-960111-99-9

HOPE
IN
HER

KRYSTA BOUQUET

To my friends and family,
all that I am is because of you and for that
I am so grateful.

CONTENTS

FOREWORD

Every teacher has those students who stand out among the rest–those who will be forever imprinted in their memory.

I spent twelve unbelievable years teaching high school students. My teaching experience included five different alternative high school programs–they're called 'alternative' because they are an alternative to the norm. However, I always felt like the way we approached it should just be the way. We had smaller class sizes, more flexibility, and more one-on-one direct instruction.

I loved teaching in this setting. I was able to see the individual learning styles of each of my students and provide them the freedom to co-create ways to best demonstrate their learning. The intimate environment gave me plenty of opportunities to get to know each of my students on a deeper level. But my favorite parts about teaching were those moments outside of the class period–the few minutes between classes, the morning before school, or most days during my prep hour–when students would visit me to talk.

I first met Krysta in 2015. She was quiet, but not in the shy high school way–quiet in the sense that she didn't care to immerse herself in the typical high school drama. She spent more time talking with her teachers and advisors than students her age. She struck me as an old soul and was wise beyond her years.

Krysta had a strong sense of purpose. She wanted to complete assignments ahead of time and was persistent in finding opportunities for extra credit where she could improve her grades. There were times when her work ethic waned and you could see the exhaustion in her eyes, but the staff and I knew why she was struggling. In our cozy little program within the high school, we were all well aware of Krysta's issues at home.

I remember my mentor informing me that Krysta was *in hiding*. We were given as much information as we needed so as not to inform anyone where she was living. As Krysta and I grew closer, she filled me in on much of the rest. I remember being in complete awe watching a young teen continually attend school and push to improve despite the chaos she was enduring outside of school. It was as if she knew her ticket out, and she was not going to let that opportunity slip by.

Krysta reached out to me again years later as an adult. I had left teaching and started a publishing company. We had stayed connected on social media, and when she contacted me to let me know she was ready to share her story, I was all in. Not only is her story one that has always stayed with me, but watching her life unfold since high school and seeing where she is today (and how she got there) is a beautiful journey that I knew needed to be shared. I couldn't wait to help bring her story to life.

Krysta's story is full of rich life lessons and a reminder that all of us are constantly growing and constantly learning. I wholeheartedly believe that the best way to do that is to hear one another's stories. When we understand the lens through which another person has had walking through their life, we can better appreciate their decisions and views on the world. Storytelling also allows us to feel inspired and to feel seen. Krysta's story does both.

There are so many nuggets in this story to walk away with, but there is an overarching message that is crucial to note. Throughout my years of teaching, I have witnessed students grow up in troubled homes. They experienced a range of trauma from neglect to substance/verbal/physical and sexual abuse. Because of their adverse childhood experiences, it was not uncommon for these students to repeat those patterns as they grew into adulthood. But it was not and is not inevitable.

Krysta was one of my students who rose above her childhood environment. She refused to carry the lineage of her family into her adulthood and made conscious decisions every day to carve out a better life for herself. Her story is proof that it is possible to change the trajectory of your life with hard work, love, and hope.

I want to speak to everyone about what I hope can be appreciated and applied after learning Krysta's story:

You are the architect of your own life. You can never control what happens to you, but you can always control what you do with it. You can choose to repeat unhealthy patterns, or you can choose to create new healthy ones. Your past can either make you jaded and keep you in a victim mentality, or it can fuel you to create a better life for yourself.

YOU are capable of so much.

Xoxo
LINDSAY BEDNAR
Krysta's Teacher/Editor/Publisher/Friend

PART 1
Hopeless

CHAPTER 1

INTO THE NIGHT

2009 is the year I lost my childhood innocence—a year that would stay in the back of my mind and on the tip of my tongue for the years to come.

It was December in northern Minnesota, where we lived in a small rural town of nearly 5,000 people. Winters here are brutal as the temps get frigid. My twin sister and I were looking forward to being out of school as we were nearing Christmas break. Year after year, we loved to convince our parents to let us open up our presents early, which had started to gather under the tree.

As joyful as this time of year is for many, we had no idea of the tailspin that was about to unravel.

The house was decorated in its normal Christmas decor, classically centered around our artificial pine tree. Our tree was adorned with homemade ornaments we kids created throughout elementary school—popsicle sticks, pipe cleaners, and sparkles littered our tree. Hanging from the mantle were five red and white stockings that were poorly decorated with every color of glitter glue. A Christmas village arranged around the fireplace was my favorite place to be. I would wait until the sun would go down to watch the little villages come to life in my living room. The little shop windows would glow, and the chapel was dressed for the holidays. It was captivating.

This was also the time of year that one of my dad's tattoos—a depiction of my sister and me wearing Santa hats at four years old—became all the more appropriate. While my mom was the type of person who carefully preserved every tooth we'd ever lost in a little box, my dad was sentimental in a different way. Besides permanently emblazing our faces on his leg, he would keep the tooth fairy alive by slipping a hundred-dollar bill under our pillow to watch our hazel eyes grow with excitement. You could say he was nostalgic in an unconventional way.

As much as Mom enjoyed Christmas, she didn't care for the long afternoons out spending money that we didn't have and battling anxiety from crowds of last-minute Christmas shoppers. It was atypical for Mom to be gone when we got home. She was a homebody through and through.

My sister Kate and I were hanging out after school, patiently waiting for Mom to get home, when the telephone rang. Back then, the only phone we had was a landline. I jumped up to grab the cordless home phone that was conveniently sitting on the edge of our green-carpeted staircase. As soon as I picked it up, I realized my dad had also picked up the phone.

"Hello?" my dad said in a gruff voice.

Without any sort of greeting, the man on the other end of the phone said, "Get your guns loaded. We're on our way."

My heart started pounding and my ears began to ring. I looked over to my sister after I hung up. I started to blurt out that someone was coming over, but before I could even finish my sentence, I heard my dad coming up the stairs. My eyes were glued to the top step to try to get a reading of his emotions. He rushed past us down the narrow hallway into the bedroom that he and my mom shared. He promptly returned with a gun. A serious and eerie tension fell over our dimly lit living room.

"Girls, I need you to go hide in the cat room," he told us with a calm urgency. His words were slow but direct. Between the gun being visible and his deliberate delivery, my body became consumed with panic.

The 'cat room' was not your typical storage closet. We called it the 'cat room' because that was where we kept the litter box—but it was used for more than just the cat. When you entered the closet, there was a small hole hiding behind the jackets that hung in the closet. It was just big enough for an adult to fit through, covered in spiders and cobwebs. Through the hole, there was a hidden area past the bins of holiday decor to a crawl space. The only time we ever really went down there was in the summer for tornado watches. Of course, using it this time was different.

The room was cold, encased with cement, and went as far out as our front steps reached. Thankfully, the green and purple *Goosebumps* comforter was always there where we left it. The space smelled like mothballs, and it was colder that day than it normally was. I felt like my body was crawling with spiders creeping amongst us. As much as we didn't want to be there, our dad made it very clear we couldn't leave until he came to get us, despite what we heard or what happened.

We lay there sprawled out on the floor. After a while, we heard people talking, but we couldn't understand anything past their muffled voices.

We looked at each other puzzled.

"Kate, what do you think is going on?" I said as I finally broke the silence. "I know it's been bad, but I don't get why we have to be down here. It's still daytime. When I picked up the phone, they said someone was on their way here and that dad needed to get a gun."

Kate piped up, "I just want to know where Mom is."

We sat and wondered where Mom was and if she was coming home anytime soon. This was more important than Christmas shopping. We didn't know where my brother was either, but a safe assumption was that he was with his friends and up to no good. Since my brother is six years older than us, he was typically always out with his friends and never home. My brother wasn't an upstanding high school boy. He was rebellious and hung around the kind of crowd your parents warned you to avoid.

After what felt like hours, I could finally see my mom's blonde hair as she peered into the cob-web-infested shelter. I leaped out of the room into my mother's warm embrace. Her heart was racing, and she kept looking over her shoulder. On the other side of the glass was nothing but the cold winter air and a dark abyss.

She shook off her fear for a second to explain to us in the simplest way possible, "I need you to pack a small bag. We're going away for a little while." A clothes pile and a dim light filled our laundry room. I looked at my reflection in the window and thought to myself: *This is a weird way to start a vacation.*

We slowly stepped up the staircase into a party of strangers—at least, they were strangers to my sister and me. My dad seemed to know every last one of them. There were countless men with badges wearing uniforms all around our house. The mood in the room felt tense like we were in a rush against time. I got overwhelmed and a little uneasy because in the past, when police officers visited us, they were never there to just say 'hi.' The sheer number of police officers on this particular visit gave me the impression that something big was happening.

As I placed my feet on the top step, I was met by a police officer. He got down on one knee and held out his gold cross necklace. His eyes met mine, and he told me that they were there to keep us safe. *Why would we need to be kept safe on vacation,* I wondered. Something just didn't feel right; I felt a little uneasy and confused. But what did I know? I was only eleven.

We packed the few things that could fit in our little bags. Since we weren't allowed to wear makeup at the time, I made sure I brought my silver eye glide shimmer eyeshadow that I had convinced my mom she needed to buy. This stuff was the best thing my eleven-year-old self owned. It was the perfect shade of silvery blue and went on my eyes smoothly.

With my bags packed and butterflies in my stomach, I slowly pressed the screen door open and saw the front of a cop car with more lined up behind it. There seemed to be an endless sea of red and blue twinkling lights. Something about this cold December night was different. The brisk wind swept over my cheeks and down the back of my jacket. It made me feel alive and simultaneously terrified.

The five of us piled into my dad's black SUV along with our three Rottweilers. The car was packed so tightly—all I could think about was our childhood cat Kelly who we had to leave behind. We started to head down our long private drive lined with pine trees, an undercover cop car in front of us and one behind us while another blocked off the highway traffic.

We slowly drove away from our house, leaving behind so much. The Christmas tree was still filled with our childhood ornaments. Presents had been wrapped, expectantly waiting to be opened, some hopefully sooner than Christmas Day. Our beds weren't made, and dishes had piled up in the sink. Clothes were strewn on the floor and the food in our fridge was left uneaten.

Where are we going? I thought.

None of this made any sense.

CHAPTER 2

A MAN ABOUT A HORSE

We drove east, heading further and further away from our small town. We stopped an hour later at a hotel where we would stay for a few nights. People came and left our room as my parents took endless phone calls. Their body language was alert—they weren't themselves. I felt so separated from them. From the moment we walked down the front steps of our house, I felt overlooked in the chaos.

My father, at times, would leave, and we'd ask where he was headed. His response would be no different than the ones he had given us over the past several years: "I'm going to go see a man about a horse." We always wondered what that meant, and as much as we wanted it to be the case, we knew it was never really about us getting a horse.

My sister and I enjoyed the sweet hotel hot chocolate in the lobby. This place was great, but it wasn't a kid-friendly hotel. Everything just looked expensive and nice. While it was kinda cool, it felt very detached. We were completely removed from our friends and school. As each day passed, so did another day of school and another day where our friends wondered where we were. It was like a whole family disappeared that December night—without a trace.

After a few days, we moved to a hotel an hour south of where we were. This hotel wasn't as fancy as the previous one, but it had many more kid-friendly amenities. There was a great restaurant, a water park with a water slide, and even a theater that hosted live plays. On top of our hotel stays, we were told that for Christmas, we were going on a trip where childhood dreams came true—Disney World. We were thrilled. While this seemed like a really weird start to a family vacation, we had never been on one, so we had nothing from which to compare it.

We settled into our room with two spacious queen beds for my mom, my sister, and me and a separate room for my dad and my brother. We were strictly told not to tell any of our friends or family where we were. We still didn't understand why this trip was so top secret and oddly planned.

The hotel breakfast had the best buttery Belgian waffle I had ever tasted. We started a daily routine of a warm, sugary breakfast and an afternoon at the waterpark. This all seemed fun until the second week hit—we were tired, our hair was brittle, and everything we owned smelled like chlorine. The days dragged on, and my parents were always watching through the little hole in the door and the windows, looking for anyone who would come close. At night, we'd get into the SUV and go shopping. This made our shopping trips more exciting, giving us a sense of freedom and adulthood being out and about after dark. My sister and I would blast Alicia Keys' *Empire State of Mind* as loud as my mom would allow. I'd close my eyes and dream of being in a big city with endless opportunities—and not 'hiding.'

Christmas was upon us. The hotel was covered in sparkly red ribbon—the kind that rubs off on you when you touch it, and the air was full of the dust from the old artificial tree. But that year, it didn't feel like Christmas. All of our presents were at home, and we didn't get to go to my grandma's house to bake home-made Russian tea cake or melting-moment cookies with her and my aunt. There were no stockings hung on the mantle with the fireplace lit. My mom went and got other gifts to fill the void of the gifts we requested. That was my mom; she always did her best to give us what she could. Although we did get to go to Grandma's on Christmas Eve, it just wasn't the same excitement that usually comes with Christmas.

A few more days went by, and this hotel was full of people ready to ring in the new year. You could hear the laughter and excitement down the halls overflowing into the water park. As the eve of the new year approached, a friend of my father joined us with his girlfriend. He was a well-dressed and cleaned-up man, not the typical type of man my dad would have around. He was a joy to have with us. We ran down the halls and rode on clunky luggage carts. We danced through the lobby and snooped in the restricted 'Staff Only' closets. We even brought back some holiday decor we scored from the lobby to bring some life into our hotel room.

As the clock struck midnight and we watched the ball drop live in New York City on the television, you could hear the hall erupt with cheering and noise makers. There's something so exciting about the start of a New Year. It's a clear slate. It was hard to be sitting in the room and not contain that same excitement. But something didn't feel right. It wasn't exactly where I thought I'd be ringing in the New Year, knowing that this 'family vacation' was being extended for who knows what reason.

As days wore on, we watched Jesse Ventura's conspiracy theories while we sat intensely in our beds. I don't remember much besides him talking about aspartame and the hidden things of the Denver airport. But I do remember my sister getting so worked up about the government trying to kill us that she cried herself into a panic attack. I still avoid aspartame to this day.

I loved the food. This place had the best buffets and chocolate covered-strawberries; this was a luxury for us. My family didn't have the most money growing up, so eating out every night was a dream come true. I didn't even mind the TV dinners–the ones with the brownies in them. I can still taste the pizza dinner with the tough and chewy crust. We would eat those often since our rooms only had a microwave and a mini fridge. But we got to watch movies and eat dinner in bed, so it was still a win-win.

We were living a real-life *Suite Life of Zack and Cody* story. At times, we thought what we got to do in a day was so cool. Living in a hotel with a water park, endless snacks, and a live theater with no school was a kid's dream, and it was becoming a sort of reality for us. The irony? The one thing we were lacking at that time was reality. The truth was, there was no impending vacation. The life that we knew was a lie.

And we had no idea that what we were about to find out would change the course of our lives forever.

CHAPTER 3

HOLLYWOOD

What was once unfamiliar became familiar quite quickly. We established our new routines, most days looking like the last. But this day was different—this was a day that would be etched in the back of my mind forever.

We were in my dad's hotel room with my brother, who was lounging near his skateboard and wearing a backwards hat. My brother was in a skater-boy phase and I love that about him. The boys' hotel room was much different than ours. The smell of cologne lingered throughout the room. The beds were left unmade, and the little wooden table in the corner was piled high with snacks for the times they got the munchies. My mom and my sister were close to me, positioned on the end of the bed.

My dad was a very expressive man—you always knew how he felt by the look on his face. At that very moment, he was quite reserved. You could see from the way that he was postured on the bed that what he was about to tell us was heavy, like the weight was almost too hard for his physical body to carry. My heart raced as he set up this conversation; my hands got clammy, and my focus kept going to my mom. I had waited through my tears and sleepless nights for this. As young as I was, I believe that through the delusion, I knew that there was so much more going on than what I was being told.

You could hear the reservation in his voice. It must be gut-wrenching to share truth where truth wasn't told before.

"I was doing something for work that put our lives in danger."

I remember the feeling that washed over me. I remember feeling so numb, as if this had to be a sick joke. My whole life, my dad never really worked, at least not a typical 9-5 job. He broke his back in a motorcycle accident when I was three, and since then, he was never the same. Wrapped up and consumed by pain and a prescription pill addiction, he spent most of his days messed up, sleeping, or seeing this 'man about a horse.'

He explained to us that he was working as a confidential informant to get bad guys off the street. I remembered my young self blurting out, "Like Perry the Platypus?"

Perry the Platypus was a character from the

Disney Channel show *Phineas and Ferb*. This character would always go undercover as a secret agent and his owners never knew. This was the only thing that I could even start to compare it to, because frankly, I didn't have the slightest clue as to what was happening to my family. All I knew at that point was that everything we had been going through was a total lie, and I didn't know what was true anymore. All I knew was that my life would never look the same.

My dad went on to explain to us that he was in a well-known motorcycle gang. My dad did things he wasn't proud of, but we all have made mistakes at some point in our lives. Still, nothing hurts like watching your child make the same decisions that you desperately wanted to keep hidden from them. I think the reality was that my dad's decisions influenced my brother's addiction, which laid a heavy burden on my dad to turn his life around—at least the best he could. It came out that someone shared my dad's name in an out-of-state court case where he was working with an agent as a Confidential Informant (CI). This information was never meant to be shared as it was known it would put us in grave danger. Because of the stage of the investigation, releasing his name would throw out everything they had worked on out the window, not to mention get us killed. They took us out that night after having intercepted a phone call with a phone tap that revealed *they* were coming for us that night— *they*, being a gang who was sending a prospect to kill us. Killing us would keep my dad from being able to testify about anything else he knew.

I tried to gather myself, but I was engulfed with fear—the type of fear that's paralyzing. So many questions filled my mind.

"What about my friends? Will I be able to go back to school? Grandma? We can't leave grandma behind," I blurted out as I tried to make sense of the situation. It was hard to think about leaving everything we knew behind us. "Is anyone else in danger?" I wondered.

My parents explained to us that we were safe. Grandma was safe. The goal was to tell the least amount of people where we were for their safety, so even our extended family members couldn't know our location. We couldn't book our hotel rooms under our real names, so the U.S Department of Justice put our reservation under the name "Rachel Weaver."

I took time alone to process the words I had just heard. My mind could not fathom the situation we were thrust into. How could anyone want to hurt us? My sister and I would often stay the night in my parents' room—we were too traumatized to sleep in our own room. Our young eyes had seen many things and experienced so much trauma that if we weren't close to my parents, we'd lay restless in our beds. The scariest thing was how easy it would have been to kill us that night with four of the five of us sleeping in the same room. The thought of it was difficult for me to get past.

So, what happens now? I thought. Someone was still out to kill my dad for a hefty reward. This was new to me too. I had no idea that people would pay someone to kill. What do you do when someone is out to kill you?

CHAPTER 4

LIFE AFTER

We left that hotel and went to stay at a house on a busy street in St. Paul near the Como Zoo. We visited the Zoo often. The mustache monkeys were one of our favorite exhibits to visit with my dad. He loved that place.

The house was cute and simple with old character. My brother enjoyed this place the most, with having many places to ride his skateboard. He stayed in the upstairs bedroom that had a window that opened up to the roof. He'd sit near the open window and feed the squirrels passing through. He had a caring heart, and was an incredible skateboarder. My brother was nearly a carbon copy of my father when it came to looks and personality.

I enjoyed being in the city as the spring was near. I'd watch the traffic go by as I lay on the hammock.

I'd enjoy the fresh spring air while snacking on a jar of Jiffy peanut butter. The spring brought a lot of hope that better days were coming—winters in Minnesota can be depressing as it is. Occasionally, we would still have men stop by to check on us and talk to my parents. One of them brought us the best fried chicken that I've ever had.

Soon, March approached, and we got to go to the St. Patrick's Day parade in St. Paul. It was crowded with people that filled the streets with a sea of green. It smelled like spilt beer, and everyone seemed to be enjoying themselves. This day brought me so much joy—a joy that would continue to bring me excitement in a season that was lonely and scary. Being away from school and having to lie to my friends was hard. I was living in a lie.

Most people had no idea how bad life really was at home. Often, my dad would say hurtful things that he didn't mean, things that would make me feel ashamed and unloved. And there would be times he'd share his aggression through physical lunges at my mom. Drugs were always around the house, and the smell of marijuana was always present—the plant could be seen growing taller than me in the backyard. At-home life up to this point wasn't only unhealthy, it was very dangerous. Going to school had been the only safe place in our lives, and we were taken from it. Being in hiding only made my dad's drug use worse as he tried to cope with constant anxiety and fear.

We were told that we were waiting to go into the Witness Protection Program. I had heard of witness protection but only from the movies. I didn't think it was a real thing. I learned that the program was designed for those whose lives were in danger for helping the US Government. My mom was in contact with the FBI and US Marshals about our placement. Once we were accepted, we would move to South Florida with a new name and a new identity. The thought of that was kinda exciting. I spent time thinking about how I would change my appearance and what I would want my new name to be. I considered what our story could be. I thought that I would go with blonde hair and change my name to something common, like Nicole.

While reinventing myself sounded exciting, I began to wonder about our family. The thought of never talking to my grandma again killed me. The notion that I would never go shopping with my aunties or enjoy their cooking again made me sad. There were so many things that I would miss. What about my friends? I would miss my little hometown.

I also knew there were things that my parents would look forward to if we went into the Witness Protection Program. All of our debt would be wiped away. This would be life-changing for my family.

Many rumors were circling at this point, one being that my dad testified fifty-two pages worth on a guy and that we were already in witness protection.

Another was that my dad stole a million dollars from the gang and was on the run. And the last was that he ripped off the gang and was in hiding. At one point, an ex-member showed up at my grandma's house asking questions—this made us all feel uneasy.

There was still someone always watching us at all times of the day. There were so many moments where it all felt like a dream, where I couldn't help but think, *This really can't be my life.*

❖ ❖ ❖

As days turned into weeks and weeks turned into several months, we wondered if we were ever going to be safe again. March came to an end, and we drove back to the first town we stayed in a little over an hour northeast of where we were.

This is the day, I told myself.

After today, we'd have clarity and safety.

An hour had passed since my parents stepped behind the wooden double doors that led into the hotel conference room. Once the doors swung open, you could see the disappointment in my dad's eyes as he walked out of the room right past us. My mom looked confused and concerned, but no one said anything. My siblings stayed close. We had no idea what this meant for us.

"We're going home," my dad said in a rush of frustration.

My dad decided to not testify, and we were going

to head home to defend ourselves. He didn't think he had to dig the hole deeper for the slight possibility of our safety. We just had to be sitting ducks waiting and hoping not to get killed. How could this be? We were all in utter disbelief. How was it possible for the government to put us through all of this to just let us go home?

We soon packed up everything that we had accumulated over the past few months. My dad and brother left to check out our house that hadn't been lived in for months. They took down some wood from the boarded windows and added extra safety measures like cameras and guns in every nook and cranny. Us girls went to go stay with my grandma and aunt until we knew it was safe to go back home.

As the school year started to come to an end for everyone back home, I began thinking about all of the things I loved about this time of year and felt excited to be a part of them, especially the track and field day that we students got to participate in. They'd give us a white shirt with track and field written on it, and you'd bring markers for all the students to sign. I remember getting so excited to pick out what color markers to bring. I'd wake up that morning so giddy to participate. This day came with the signing of the yearbooks, which was my favorite part because I loved words of affirmation. I didn't get it at home, and at school, this made me feel so loved. I'd often read them over and over again. As scared as I was to go home, I still had many things to look forward to.

It was the first day back for my sister and me, and my classmates' faces lit up with pure excitement when we arrived. Because a kid in my grade had a parent in one of the gangs, we got all our friends to believe that we were in Arizona taking care of a sick relative. We couldn't trust other kids with the knowledge of where we were, and truthfully, they wouldn't understand. I felt both nervous and relieved to have some normalcy. But we quickly learned how curious sixth graders can be as we were bombarded with a million questions:

"Where were you?"

"Why were you gone for so long?"

"Are they okay?"

"Did you go to school while you were gone?"

As annoying as it was, it was a relief to be back.

I opened up my locker that I hadn't touched in months, wondering, "*Where do I even pick up?*" I will be honest, it felt nice to just be seen in these first few days of being home. I desperately desired to just be with people I knew and loved because it wasn't something that was promised to me at that time. It never is to anyone, but for us, we learned that lesson early.

School came with another fear. Anytime the phone rang or our names were called at the end of the day to come down to the office, my heart would race. There was this fear rising within me of "What's Next?" or "What Now?" There was an anticipation that something bad was going to happen.

And there was also an awkwardness of being home. We were told that no one, not even our teachers were allowed to know what we just went through. I felt like I was living a double life. I so badly wanted someone to know what I had just gone through. After the trauma and pain we experienced, everyone simply thought that we were visiting a sick relative. How do you even recover from living such a lie?

CHAPTER 5

SUMMER 2010

The year came to a screeching halt, and we left for summer break. We had a friend of ours that moved to Tucson, Arizona. While we were in hiding, my parents reached out and planned for my sister and me to go out there for the summer. The plan was that our family friend would drive up to pick us up, and my parents would come out to pick us up at the end of summer. This trip was such a relief for us, but at the same time, I couldn't help but call home crying. All I knew was dysfunction, and I craved chaos. I wrestled between the warmth of feeling safe and the unknown of going home. When you're home, you don't always see how bad life is until you leave. Even though I could see clearly how messed up things were at home, I missed the fear of the unknown, because at that point, it was all I've ever known.

The weather was warm in Tuscon, our skin was tan, and my medium brown hair was a lived-in blonde by the time our stay came to an end (thanks to all the fresh lemons we juiced on our heads). We spent most of our time laying by the pool; it was everything we needed—rest and a good night's sleep. It was hard because I missed home. I didn't miss everything about home, just some things. I often wondered if I did miss the chaos, or if that's what "Normal" had become for me and I just liked consistency.

We ate these little gelato bites like it was nobody's business as we watched the little geckos climb the adobe houses. We would spend our weekends at Mount Lemon looking for all the cool cacti on the way up. I adored this little ghost town attraction where you got to go panning for gold. I think I just enjoyed the thrill of searching for something that you rarely can find; it made it that much better when you did find it—although I was convinced they put the fake flakes of gold in there to keep people coming back.

Our friend's dog had pappy-wawa puppies, half chihuahua and half papillon. I cried like a baby until my parents let me pick one out to take home with me. I picked out this sweet little white and tan puppy and named her Peanut. In my defense, my parents were lucky that I even agreed to come back to their crazy home. I think a puppy was a fair deal.

The summer quickly came to an end, and our family met us in San Diego. This was the first time our family has ever taken a real vacation together. We met at Sea World and watched the live shows while getting drenched by seawater. We soon left with our new puppy and headed up to Hollywood where they dropped my brother off the night before. We got to the motel where he was staying with his friends. This room was a cheap motel room that looked bug infested and smelled like drugs. The pillows were all over the room, and my brother and his friends hadn't even gotten up yet and it was close to lunchtime. We got them cleaned up and went to check out Venice beach and the little stars that lined the ground that the city is famous for. It was truly so nice to be able to spend some time as a family, and even though I knew they couldn't afford this trip, I think they were experiencing some parental guilt.

We started our journey driving home, and that came with an uneasy feeling of uncertainty. Life was so much better when we knew we don't have to worry about a thing. I loved being able to spend time as a family after what we had all been through, but to go back to our normal lives was terrifying. The car ride was quiet. I think we all had an understanding of what we were going home to.

Soon, we were back home again—the house was looking great now that the windows were unboarded and a new deck was built in the backyard. Being home made me feel uneasy, but it didn't stop my sister and I from being kids. The neighbor boy next door was our best friend, and we'd spend the rest of the days playing baseball or building a fort. As the sun would set, we'd scurry inside.

I loved sharing a room with my sister so we wouldn't have to sleep alone, even though we always had one of our four dogs with us. These weren't your typical family dogs—three of them were Rottweilers that were there for protection. If my dad would yell at us or get mad, they would come in front of us and protect us. The dogs were the ones who took the brunt force of my dad's rages. I often wondered whether we'd be the ones to take it if they weren't there. If a friend would get close or try to hug us, they would give them a warning nip. These dogs were how I rested at night knowing that they would be on my front-line defense against my dad and those who were after us. I couldn't imagine life without them.

As I lay my head down at night with my window cracked, I would worry. It was always a struggle. Do I leave it open in case I need to jump out? Or do I lock it so no one can come in? Do I leave it cracked so I can hear outside? Every night looked so different depending on what I was anxiously worried about. I struggled with sleeping for many years as a child and a teen because of this. It was emotionally draining to be afraid of both the outside and the inside of my home—I never knew which side was safer.

I would fear that I wouldn't wake up again or that someone would have an overdose while I was sleeping, which sadly did happen. I would often be jolted out of my sleep by my mother crying and screaming for help. 911 was always quick to come, and time and time again, they would save my brother. Each time, I was left scarred by the picture of his nearly lifeless body and the blood-curdling screams of my mom.

My brother was away for a lot of my childhood. He was constantly in and out of treatment. During holidays, I would sob, just wanting my older brother that I looked up to. As I got older, I desired to learn how to skateboard like him. I thought he was so cool and was so proud to have him as my brother. It killed me to know that he was also wrapped in addiction. But addiction isn't anything new for my family—it's something that my dad's mom also struggled with and introduced my father to at an early age.

I would hear the roaring of the packs of motor-cycles that would circle our house, taunting us. Some got as bold as to pull down our long private drive. I would leap off the bed and press my face against the window as my heart raced and my breath got heavier. It could be as small as a helicopter flying above, a car coming down the driveway, or a bush moving—I was always alert and ready to run for my life.

* * *

After the fall came back around, my dad reached out to a well-known local news station, and a well-known reporter came to our house to report on our story. The piece was going to shed light on the corruption of the task force. The corruption was complex, as it involved an out-of-state court case.

As a CI, my dad was sent to Missouri to offer insight into another chapter of his same gang. One of the task force officers in Missouri wanted to wrap up his case and consequently used my dad's testimony. They knew that there was danger in releasing his name, and they did it anyway. This was not the plan that was in place to keep my dad safe as it outed him as a snitch. Not only was it not the plan, but it also wasn't approved, and it definitely wasn't legal. It compromised the operation to keep our family safe, which led to the discussion of the Witness Protection Program.

The Task Force, FBI, the US Marshals, and even the IRS came together on this case. They intercepted a phone call that gave them insight. On the night of December 16, 2009, a prospect from the gang was going to come to take the lives of everyone in my family.

This story exposed a task force that fell in Minneapolis due to corruption happening within its own walls and in the city of Minneapolis. This wasn't going to be a one-time interview but something that was going to be an ongoing investigation. They covered my dad's face and showed different parts of our house, like the bathtub we were often forced to hide in if things started to get dicey. A few days after it was aired, they ended up taking it down from all media platforms that it could be found on, and we were told that there was no more story. This was hard to hear, my parents wanted nothing more than answers. Understandably, they shut it down—the people behind the decisions that put our lives in danger didn't want the truth to be told.

To think that someone was sent to my home to kill us stirs something up within me. It still haunts me to this day. I've wrestled for years with fears and anxiety. Missing my friends and school was devastating. I would be on edge for the years to come.

* * *

As I got older, things started clicking. I vividly remember these men that were out to get us. They always referred to my dad as "Hollywood," which wasn't a surprise if you saw the rest of them. They were some of the roughest looking men I'd ever seen, but my dad was a well-groomed, cleanly dressed man.

Dad was not your typical family man. His body was covered in other people's artwork that he had collected over the years, and he looked like a man you wouldn't want to cut off in midday road rage. But he was indeed good-looking; his dark chestnut hair was slicked back smoothly with gel that would harden in place. Beyond his good looks, he was utterly intriguing. He possessed something that drew you into him, always leaving you wanting to know more. He had a sense of humor that would bring me to tears with laughter. When he was mad, however, he was the scariest person on this side of hell.

While charming and good-looking from the outside, he was very unpredictable. It was hard at times to know if it was the drugs or if he was truly bipolar. His emotions were often all over the place, resulting in him quickly lashing out. One minute, he'd be looking as healthy as could be, and in another, he'd look like he had one foot in the grave. Whatever the cause, he never really got help for it; he just suppressed it with more drugs. He knew what he needed to do and say at the exact moment to get what he wanted—or he'd fake a heart attack to get it. Working with the police got him out of a lot of trouble. For years, I prayed that he'd get in trouble for doing drugs, but the protection gave him an allowance to keep doing it.

I knew what drugs were at a very young age, and as I got older, his use only continued to get worse. It started with weed and progressed to pills. Not long after, I started finding spoons with weird powder on them and orange caps from a syringe on the bathroom floor. I would often look throughout the house only to find bags of pills stuffed in couch cushions and pillowcases. Old prescription bottles were commonly found with weed stashed inside of them.

There would be times my brother would be distraught that a girl would be "shooting up" and would say so many ungodly things about her. A few weeks later, I'd catch her hanging out at our house. That's when I started to see more caps. I often wondered if that was his way of trying to get me to believe that he wasn't doing some of the things that they were doing.

All throughout my childhood I would go to school smelling like weed, and it was devastating to have people question my character. I learned that your choices do affect other people, so choose wisely. Because they made the decision to smoke, I reaped the consequence of their decisions. I was associated with them and directly affected by it. It was hard because I was close to my mom, but my mom was lost in all of it, trying to save my dad and brother and protect us.

CHAPTER 6

LINGERING LIES

As I reflect on the past several years, there are common themes that I've noticed—dysfunction and too many lying tongues. At the time, I didn't know it, but I was living a life harboring lies for my parents. There were many situations where things were greatly wrong, but I was exposed to them as being "normal."

Hesitantly, I looked back on what I thought was a normal childhood. When I was born, we lived in Crystal, Minnesota—a little suburb of Minneapolis. At the end of our block was a barbed-wire fence that lined the Crystal Airport. As a little girl, I'd watch the small two-passenger planes take off and land. I remember that once a year, the airport grounds would be filled with clowns and bright colors as the circus would pass through, which left me staying inside my house all weekend long.

My twin sister and I would play house and make homemade mud pies in our fenced backyard. This one-story yellow home was quaint, but in the spring, it became vibrant with pops of pink that would cover the front yard stemming from the cherry blossom tree. Down the street, as you headed away from the airport, lived the sweetest lady; her house had a warm vanilla scent and had the most well-dressed dollhouse I have ever seen. The dollhouse looked like I could reside in it. Her home was well lived in and always had the outdated colorful hard candies. She would often look forward to our visits, and so would we.

Across the street from us lived a nice family. Their father was a local fireman. One day, when I was four years old, I was up in the cherry blossom tree with my brother when I fell backward out of it head first onto the ground. I remember my head hitting the ground and my vision blurred. My brother screamed for my mom, and she ran across the street to get the fireman neighbor who was trained for these types of incidents. He checked me over and sent me inside to rest. I remember the fear and the terror that over-came me. I was filled with confusion as I lay in my parents' bed and the fireman shone a little round light in my eyes.

Those days hold vivid memories, but there was one day in particular that changed our family's story. My dad was gone a lot during the day when us kids were growing up. My mom worked part-time, and my dad was always out doing something. This day was warm from the sun shining through the windows, and the air was crisp. It was a typical day for us. Suddenly the phone rang, and my mom screamed.

"Oh my gosh, oh my gosh!" my mom yelled over and over again. She stood still and her eyes filled with fear. Frantically, my mom threw the phone down and called a neighbor to come over until Bobbie Jo, my dad's mom, could watch us.

We never called her 'Grandma' because we didn't really view her as one. She was never loving and caring like our other grandma. My mom's mom was kind and welcoming, and her home always was cozy and smelled like freshly baked cookies. She kept our favorite ice cream treats on hand, and she always had our favorite bread that would use to make us buttered toast. My dad's mom, on the other hand, lived in what looked and smelled like a crack house.

One time, when I was really young, she took me to the water park and put me down a big slide by myself, and I almost drowned. I remember the panic that came over my body as I could only see the splashing water. A lifeguard saved me and scolded her. Let's just say that after that, she was only able to watch us by herself in true emergencies.

So, on the day of the accident, Mom raced out the door and into our silver minivan, leaving us with a distant neighbor only to be filled by the incompetent shoes of Bobbie Jo. Mom left in a hurry, and we felt uneasy. She didn't come home for hours, and when she did, she looked like hell.

The accident was terrible. My dad was riding home on his motorcycle, and when he put his hand out to signal his turn, another driver wasn't paying attention and hit him. The driver panicked, backed up, and hit him again. Most people picturing this happening would imagine the driver as distracted and young. Some would assume the driver was on their phone. It was actually an ambulance driver that hit him. It's still hard for me to wrap my head around this.

Dad was in the hospital for many weeks undergoing unimaginable pain and multiple surgeries. He had always been addicted to drugs since he was young, but this opened a new door to make it "okay." Before his accident, he'd often have me on his bike with him. He enjoyed plopping me on the front of the seat and taking me for a whirl around the neighborhood. As much as I loved these memories, I can no longer see them through the innocence I once had. Now all I can see are the lies, the deception, and the gateway that this injury caused.

CHAPTER 7

I have so many memories of things being not quite right as a child. When you're little, whatever your environment is feels normal. As an adult, I look back on these situations and can't imagine subjecting a child to them.

DARK & DINGY:

My little hand held a tight and sweaty grip on my dad as we walked into a blocky old building lined with motorcycles parked in the front. It was dark; I couldn't see much with poor street lighting. Adjacent to the building, I could see the skyline of the city.

I knew that we had been in the car for a while as this looked nothing like home. As we entered this warehouse-type building, I was smacked in the face with a horrible smell. It smelled like an ashtray and liquor. The men there were towering over me and they look like the men that you'd often see sitting under the bridges along the highway. The room was dark, and it had a darts machine and old bar games in the front corner. This place had a bar feel, yet it wasn't a bar.

I plopped on a red-topped ripped bar stool and dangled my feet. My dad was pretty occupied with the guys and let me know that he was going to step away for a second. Each person who passed by was dripping with red and black dressings, most of which were leather. I heard the chains that they wore cling and clang while bikes outside started to rev up their engines. I wasn't sure where we were or what my dad was doing, but what I did know was that this place made me nervous.

A LITTLE UNSTEADY

As my dad's battle began to increase, my mom's strength lessened by the day.

She lived her whole life taking care of everyone but herself. This sucked the life out of her; my dad sucked the life out of her.

One day, my dad was slumped over on the couch, as he often was, mumbling things I wasn't able to understand. Concerned, I rushed over to him and asked, "What was that?" This only made him more irritable.

"Dammit, Krys, I didn't say anything to you," he spewed back angrily.

As I got older, it became more of a game to mess

with him. With his head bobbing around and his coordination compromised, Dad was attempting to eat a bowl of cereal. During one of his elongated blinks, my sister and I decided to put a little paper ball in his cereal to see if he'd eat it. When he did, we squealed with laughter.

"What the hell are you two dipshits laughing at?" He didn't even know that he ate it.

Laughter is supposed to fill a young person's childhood, but not mine. Laughter made my dad's whole body cringe. He would get enraged every time I laughed as a child. He always seemed to internalize that the laughter was directed at him. This has followed me into adulthood, at times making it hard for me to laugh, let loose, and have fun.

Dad's patterns became all too familiar. He'd get all his pills at the beginning of the month and binge until he could barely function. After he had either taken too many pills or sold them for profit, he'd run out at the end of the month, making him terrifying to be around. He'd yell profanities and punch the walls. Our house was covered in holes from all of his rages, one time leaving a can of beans wedged into the kitchen wall. His frustration all too often came out sideways, ending in an injured yelp from our dogs.

His aggression made me submissive and reserved. It muted me. It caused me to retreat to my bedroom.

We always knew when he was angry. His usually light blue eyes would get a yellow-gold line through them—a symptom, I later learned, that is synonymous with addiction. They say the eyes are a gateway to the soul, and when he was on something and angry, he appeared to be soulless.

THE FAMILY BUSINESS:

Our house was in a sweet little town an hour north of Minneapolis. It was known for nothing good, leaving people up to nothing good. When I'd walk through the screen door into our house, I'd often get a waft of marijuana coming up from the basement. This smell often came with me as I left, leaving me in uncomfortable situations at school. At the tender age of five, I was very aware of what drugs were.

One day, the neighbor boy approached me and said, "Your brother and your dad are potheads."

It stopped me in my tracks, and I tried to defend against their drug use.

"No, they're not!"

"Yeah, they are! They're growing marijuana in the backyard!"

My instinct was to defend them, even though I knew they were guilty of what they were being accused of.

Many years went by, and it only became more evident what was truly happening. It first started as a personal addiction and eventually became a family business. We were told if we kept quiet, the plants growing would be our Christmas presents.

These plants were like nothing I had ever seen before. I looked up to see the tops of them. I hated these plants. They smelled like skunk and often led to a lot of ongoing issues. Often, there were times when my brother raced into the house and one of us was told to be on the lookout.

"They're pulling down the driveway!" we shouted one day, peeking from behind the curtain.

The whole family ran to the backyard, lit a fire, and started burning all the plants as a black and white car slowly came to a stop. My brother was up to no good when a cop caught wind of it, leading the family to go into full-blown panic mode, burning the evidence.

Another time, I heard my brother yelling out the back door, stumbling down to the basement as he breathlessly went into his room to grab something. As he flung open the front door, he screamed, "We're being robbed, Mom! We're being robbed!"

Naturally, I sprang into an adrenaline rush and ran out the front door in step with him. I wasn't as prepared for it as he was and had no idea what someone would possibly want to steal from us. We rushed past our large oak tree with the rope swing to the field just behind our house. A girl was suspiciously lounging in the field thirty feet in front of us. My brother whipped out a gun and pointed it at the little blonde.

I immediately put my focus on my brother as he yelled ungodly words to the girl, waving the gun around like it was his other hand. Frantically my instincts kicked in.

"You need to put the gun down. This isn't worth it. She isn't worth it. You wouldn't dare do this in front of me."

He piped back, "Kid, you need to get out of here and let me take care of this."

Finally, my mom came running across the yard. Frantically, she yelled, "Stop, you don't want to do this. Don't do this in front of your sister." It was broad daylight with four neighbors' houses in full view of this fiasco. He finally put his illegal weapon away and tried to retrieve my 'Christmas present'.

Mom called the police. She reported that someone stole from our property and was in the possession of weed. The police showed up searching behind the local bowling alley and caught them on the run. There were two of them working together to steal the pot plant. A guy took off ahead of her with the plant. Of course, this led to round two of hiding these plants, because what they stole was illegal anyway.

This wasn't the only time there had been this type of excitement at our house. Many fights and cop calls later, it became our normal. Cars would come and go all hours of the night. This family business didn't have normal hours and only had very broken and damaged customers—people who were poorly dressed, smelly, and extremely skinny.

With the unsteadiness that came with this

addictive lifestyle, I was left alert and ready for anything that could happen. All these things were very
much so "normal." I would often be concerned and
feel weird if trouble wasn't happening. I thrived on
the chaos.

CHAPTER 8

LAND OF LAKES

In the summer, Minnesota natives love enjoying many of the 10,000 lakes that the state is known for. Growing up, we would often go to a property that was only about fifteen minutes from our home. I would hear the left blinker come on and see the red and black flame mailbox. Before long, we'd curve along the trees to a secluded home and pole barn. This cozy and masculine home belonged to a dear friend of my father's.

The house had the perfect koi pond to the left of the two-story home. This pond wasn't much bigger than a small car and was surrounded by large rocks. My sister and I would chase each other around it and search in the midday sun for any creature we could get our hands on. Most days, it would be slimy frogs enjoying a swim, and sometimes, we were lucky to get our hands on a turtle.

This place was owned by a 'good guy.' He and my dad built bikes together. There was a significant difference between the guys that my dad used to hang out with that wore red and black attire to the 'good guys'—these men didn't have colorful language like the others. They still looked dirty and rev their engines from sun up to sun down, but these ones went to church locally.

We started attending their services in a strip mall that lined the main drag in the small little town that we moved to when I was five years old. They'd sing songs about Jesus, and I would even lift my hands to join them in worship. I could feel these sensations come over my body and a sense of peace wash over me. I will never forget what I felt in those moments.

I will never forget when I found out who these people truly were.

These people were no better than the ones that wore red and black leather. They did horrible things and associated with the same crowd, eventually joining the gang that my dad was in and, subsequently, they cut off our relationship with them. We all felt bitterness and betrayal. We trusted this man, and then he became one of 'them.' Being so close to these people for many years still makes me cringe.

CHAPTER 9

HOLIDAY MADNESS

One Christmas, my dad took us shopping at Macy's in downtown Minneapolis. We always used to go down there for the Holidazzle parade. This year, we went down there early and walked around to see all the Christmas displays. After walking around for a while, we needed to use the bathroom. He walked us to the bathroom, and my sister and I walked into the ladies' room. A few minutes later, we walked out, and panic washed over us as my dad was nowhere to be found.

"Dad! Dad!" we kept yelling.

A young man approached us and started describing my dad to us. Horrified, we ran out of the store to see that my dad was pinning a guy down on the ground and a gun was laying in the middle of the street. This is in broad daylight, and a crowd started to form around him. Of course, he whipped out his badge, and Macy's security called the police. This guy that my dad had on the ground was robbing Macy's, and when he ran past, my dad jumped into action. It was a relief, of course, to find out that the gun belonged to my dad. The police came and took the man away, and my dad should have walked away with an award. That's the type of guy that my dad was—always ready to hop into whatever came his way. Let's just say our city adventures with my dad were very few and far between—I think it was per my mom's request, especially after that midday cops and robbers incident.

My dad was also a bounty hunter for a while. I'm not entirely sure what that entailed, but I know he'd pick up bad guys in the most bizarre ways. My dad always had that vest with him, which only made me want one—not a black one but a pink one. Growing up, I always told him that if he wanted to get me anything, it would be a pink gun and a pink bulletproof vest. My dad's investment into going after bikers and bad guys sprung up a desire for me at one point to do the same. I wanted to follow in his footsteps because I loved the thrill of it. I loved the chaos. But not too long after I had this desire, it quickly left. I wanted my life back. I wanted to trade my chaos for peace.

CHAPTER 10

HOPE IN HER

Almost a year had passed since we went into hiding and life went back to how it was before we left. A few of our friends from the church we had been attending invited us to a retreat. This wasn't like the biker church—it was a real church with good-hearted people.

I was first introduced to the church when I was in the third grade. Our school partnered with a local church through a program called RELEASE time. This program allowed a student with a parent's permission to leave school for an hour to learn about Jesus. This was something I wasn't very familiar with, but a few kids in my class were going.

My parents let us attend this retreat with the local church called Breakaway, an opportunity for students to "break away" from school and at-home life. This sounded like everything I needed and more.

As the weekend approached, we got the devastating news that a boy my age in our youth group passed away in a car accident. As we left for the weekend, we spent time praying for his family and gathered around his sibling that joined us a day later. This moved my heart, having compassion and empathy as they dealt with unimaginable pain. I got to witness the level of community and comfort that the church offered.

This weekend was the same one I found myself at the altar down on my knees accepting Jesus Christ as my personal Savior. It was a pivotal point for me; I received a hope I didn't know that I could have. I remember the overwhelming emotions that washed over me that weekend: the fear of my family, not wanting to go home, but also a vivid memory of the great strength that started welling up inside of me.

Church became a regular part of my life. Every Wednesday night, and soon after, every Sunday morning, I would be at church. From serving in the coffee shop to Sunday school, I couldn't get enough of the love these people were pouring out. Our youth pastor was exactly what our church needed to lead the next generation. He led with humility and often moved me to tears with his words. His heart was evident through all he did and the team that he led. He would preach, and his emotions flowed through the sermons often making me feel like, "Wow, God really sees me right now." He and his team ministered to me on nights when I didn't want to go home.

I would meet with them often and, despite being afraid, I opened up about what my home life looked like. Their eyes wide and hearts torn, I could tell by their response that this was far from normal.

We knew that with my dad's CI work and many attempts to leave home that this was going to be a process to keep my sister and I safe. I desperately wanted to leave home, and a woman at church would often encourage me.

"In a few years, you'll be eighteen, and life will look so different for you. You will be able to make these decisions for yourself."

But I could not imagine four more years of living in constant fear. I'd cry myself to sleep and pray to God asking him to deliver me from the mess. My prayers would often sound like this:

"Lord, I pray that you give me the strength to overcome my trials. Give me eyes to see and ears to hear you. I pray that these trials would bring you honor and glory by helping those who are struggling. Break my heart for what breaks yours. My heart longs to see you move. Lord, let me in on what you're doing in my life and the lives around me. Lord, I trust you."

But there were many simple prayers, too.

Lord, deliver me.

Lord, free me from this.

Lord help me, I can't do this.

Lord, I don't understand what you're doing, but I trust you.

Many nights, I reached out to him with no words, clenching my pillow and swirling in all of my emotions.

For months, I would take pictures and videos of the drugs and drug use to try to build a case. My sister and I wanted to be careful not to put ourselves in danger with our family, but we also wanted to ensure that we'd be able to leave and not have to return.

This made school especially hard. I struggled greatly with academics and simply showing up to school. I was depressed, living in baggy clothes, and constantly tired. Being tired became something that I hid behind.

"How are you?" many would ask.

All I would have to say was, "I'm good, I'm just tired," while rubbing the side of my nose with the inside of my index finger—a little tic I did when I was nervous. This behavior was a result of my depression. I would just desire to get as much sleep as I could. Going to friends' houses gave me the ability to sleep for hours peacefully.

After six months, I was convinced I had enough to get out until the unthinkable happened. One night, I woke up from my dad yelling at my mom in the hallway. My sister and I slipped out of bed only to hear my dad spewing nasty things about my mother and stating, "If you girls weren't here, your mom would already be dead on the front steps."

My body tensed up, and my only focus was on my mom. My dad made us reluctantly go to our room without Mom, and one of our dogs followed. It was in the dead of the night, and he came into our room with the home phone and my mom's cell phone. He took the two phones and broke them right in front of us. He sat on our bed and said, "I'm not going anywhere, and if you run or call for help, I'll shoot you."

My mom was beside herself, and my brother was sound asleep in the basement. My dad stared at each of us for hours until dawn. Once my brother woke up, he went straight into a fistfight with my dad, and us girls made a run for it. Left right, left right I can remember my feet quickly hitting the grass as I ran for my life, constantly looking back to make sure he wasn't aiming a gun at us. My heart was racing, and all I could think about was my brother being in the middle of this mess while we tried to get help. We broke into our neighbors' house and called 911.

My dad hopped into his black Tahoe and got into a high-speed police chase until they cornered him in a cornfield. The police pulled us girls into questioning, and my mom told us to tell them that we don't know what happened and that we were sleeping.

I did what I was told.

I hopped into the front seat of the squad car and told the sweet little lie like my momma wanted me to, knowing full well that he was about to get away with all of it.

It wasn't long after that incident that he became furious with rage again. This time, I had had enough.

I had never stood up to my dad, but this was it. He got into my mom's face, and I told him, "You need to back up right now."

I remember when he got in my face and I dialed 911 as my dog sat alert at my feet, keeping my dad at bay. My brother smacked my phone out of my hand, and I ran out of the house. Dad met me on the landing of our steps. I looked him in the eye and said, "It's me or the drugs." He laughed in my face. At that moment, I knew it was over.

It was a Wednesday night, so I waited for my ride to church at the neighbors' house. That night, I made a decision that I was over the toxic lifestyle of abuse. I talked to my youth leaders and listened to the message as I wrestled with my thoughts. I sat in the middle of a group of high school girls who always made me feel so loved.

8 p.m. hit, and I remember a few youth leaders pulled me out of service early. They led me down the hallway to a little back room where we were met by a few police officers. I explained to them what happened. My dad and brother had a warrant out for their arrest. My dad made threats, and my brother interfered with a 911 call.

I remember when the officer looked me in the eye and told me that I didn't have to go home.

My sister and I stayed with a local foster family from church that night. I remember hopping in their car feeling afraid, not knowing what was going to happen next. My brother and dad ended up in the local newspaper for being on the "lam." The article explained how my dad was going to "shoot up" the church. I was horrified when it was published. I felt ashamed to walk through the doors of the church knowing that my dad said those awful things, and that so many people would read his words, but I was also fearful that he may be crazy enough to do it.

That was the day that I made a decision that I wasn't going to go back home, and since I was fifteen, no one made me.

That was the day I decided I was going to create a life far greater than the life that I was living, no matter what it cost.

My faith gave me a strength that I never had before, a boldness I needed, and hope for this new life. I was relieved to not be at home. I could lay my head down and sleep peacefully. I could focus on school and my job at the local breakfast café.

A family friend lent me a car and taught me for hours on end how to drive. Soon I passed my permit test. I was finally able to act my age, and I was grateful for that. After spending so many years completely consumed by chaos, I struggled to talk, mingle, and relate to kids my age. When I would start to share what I was walking through with my friends, they'd have no words. This caused me to want to stay quiet. I felt alone. I always felt like a Debby Downer. I found that what helped me the most with coping with these emotions was helping other people who were struggling.

In my small hometown, there was never a shortage of people dealing with difficult times. Suicides, drug overdoses, and car accidents took the lives of many students over the years. I had so much compassion for those walking through the fire, for I was constantly living in one.

CHAPTER 11

FROM IMPOSSIBLE TO POSSIBLE

Not too long after my dad and my brother turned themselves in, the county put out a no-contact order between my sister and I against our dad. As hard as it was, it was the best thing for all of us. I know it was hard for my mom because she still loved my dad, but legally, he couldn't live at the house, so he moved back to northeast Minneapolis. I struggled through this season with the thought that "I did this to my dad and my brother." As much as they hurt me, I still felt guilty for getting them in trouble. This made me even more fearful of them—I knew they were mad. They never expected us to speak up. As hard as it was, I was grateful for the strength and courage I had to do so.

The hardest thing after leaving home was mustering up the strength to finish high school. I was thankful that our school offered floral classes. I took these classes every semester, and it became a passion of mine. I would find myself in the greenhouse for a few hours every day by myself. It was a warm place in the winter to take a few minutes to remind myself that this was going to take time. Day after day, I grew closer to finding what my heart was longing for—a family.

My faith continued to grow as well as my voice. Being told I had to be quiet all those years and cover up everything with lies made it very hard to speak out after I left. I was trained to be quiet, but I was determined to share my story.

I made a promise to God that every time I was asked to share my story, I would never turn it down. And at a young age, I saw him use it again and again in the most unexpected places. Sharing it brought healing to me, and I got to see the Lord use it to minister to others. My church family became my biggest support and the family I never had. They cried with me, opened their doors for me, and loved me like no other. They believed in me, and they risked a lot for me. Forever I'm grateful for those who spoke up for me when I didn't have a voice. My sleepless nights and my prayers in the form of many tears were answered.

By no means was I an innocent Christian girl who did nothing bad. I grew up in a family of non-believers and drug addicts, and there were no rules. Even at the age of fifteen, I found myself sipping a wine cooler at a friend's house. One thing led to another, and it turned into a small partying spree. I do mean small—I could count how many weekends I partied on two hands. As fun as it was at the time, I knew that there was so much more to life than drinking and hiding from the cops on the weekends.

Growing up in a rural Minnesota town, there wasn't much else to do on the weekends besides drinking in a field with your friends. And once you start to hang out with that crowd, it's hard to leave— there was always another party scheduled. The nights that I partied often left me scared of being taken advantage of, so I'd lock myself in a room alone, or I'd sleep in my car with the doors locked until I could drive home in the morning. I'd be in a room full of people and still feel so alone. I knew that the only reason I was drinking was to try to fill a void in my heart that only Jesus could fill.

I had two relationships that were sinful and weren't Godly. I wrestled with dating relationships and even relationships with guy friends. The lack of not having any male figures in my life left me extremely broken. I desperately desired one thing—I just wanted to be held. I'd have sleepovers with guys and wouldn't do anything with them, not even kiss them. I just simply want to be held and not fall asleep alone. I hated being alone at night. All my fears would creep in when I was alone, which led to many sleepless nights.

Over the years, that desire to be held didn't

go away. I would go to sleep with the picture in my mind of Jesus holding me. To know and to rest in the thought that he is carrying me changed everything. I didn't desire to be loved by any of these men. What I desired more than anything was to know a father's love.

Although I had this hope welling up inside of me, it was not an instant change. It was a slow change that happened with each individual decision to do the right thing. I leaned in and listened to every message and sermon. I was in my Bible and meeting with Godly mentors to work through the pains of my past. I needed to give myself space and an overflowing amount of grace to be where I was. I needed time to process and heal, to dream and plan for this life I so greatly wanted. I needed to find the freedom to call these things out for what they were—strongholds. These holds kept me in bondage and did not want me to break these generational curses. Through my decision, I believe that the next generation of my family will be free from abuse and addiction, breaking a vicious family cycle.

Leaving home wasn't possible without the people in my life that spoke life over me. These voices positioned and prepared me to make the hard "yes" decisions that changed everything for me. By the power of the Holy Spirit at work inside of me and by the grace of God, leaving home at eighteen quickly turned to leaving home at fifteen in a blink of an eye.

The local church is the best hospital in the city. They see more people walk through the doors banged up and mangled in the messes that sin has caused in their life. I'm grateful for those who saw the warning signs and were willing to shake Heaven and Earth for me to find freedom. After hours of prayers, tears, and phone calls, I was freed from what I could see in the physical, but what I was wrestling with was spiritual. It was a slow change. My transformation would take many years to unravel.

The church is the best place to find a community to rally around you and help you to walk toward healing and freedom.

CHAPTER 12

I WANTED OUT

There are a few pages that I wanted to leave out of this book. While I was home, the Lord reminded me of my heart behind this book. I want to be real. I want to be honest.

I'm not trying to paint a pretty picture of my life; I want to let you into the messiest parts of it.

When I was in the first few years of high school, I struggled with depression. I was so sad to not have my dad in my life. I missed him more than I could ever imagine. When I was in my early years of high school, I was struggling. I was in an ungodly relationship with a guy that I was convinced I was going to marry one day.

I ended up talking to my dad on the phone when I legally wasn't supposed to.

That next day, I wanted to end my life. I didn't

want a life living in constant fear. I started believing the lies that the enemy was telling me.

"I'm not enough."

"I'm not loved."

"It's better if I'm not here."

I went to my mom's house and grabbed a bottle of Ibuprofen and took as many as I could and texted my mom. I didn't do any research; I just took what I could find.

My mom rushed home and took me to the hospital. We got there, and I threw up. They took my mom out of the room to talk to me. I was desperate. I wanted out. I wanted to be freed from the lies that the enemy was telling me. I didn't want to die; it was a cry for help. I talked to a doctor, and they released me that night.

This is a part of my story that I don't talk about often. It feels like it happened a lifetime ago. I haven't felt that way since that day. I didn't want to end my life; I was just dying to get out of the mess I was living in. I wanted my dad in my life. What I desired more than anything was a father's love. Fortunately for me, I ended up finding that in the Lord.

CHAPTER 13

CARRIED

The word that comes to mind when I look back on the past several years is "carried." It is as if my feet were not moving on my own accord, but as if the Lord carried me through it all. It was not my own strength or discernment that protected me. When I look back, I see his fingerprints all over it.

From RELEASE time to my hand lifted high at the little biker church, I see that it was him all along. His protection and provision have followed me and relentlessly pursued me. Each time I'm reminded of his faithfulness, and this stirs my soul. When a trial would come, I'd remember the overcoming victory in the last one. In the uncertainty, he would give me peace. In the fear, he'd give me strength. In the depths of loneliness, he sent a warm embrace that surrounded me. And after it was over, he'd show me how great my faith is in him—each time believing and knowing that he'd do it again.

If I could go through all these things, then surely, I have nothing to fear. He's been faithful and, rest assured, he will continue to be. When I look back to the days when I was in the worst of it, I'm often reminded of the story in Daniel 3, where there was a king who demanded everyone to bow down to him, and if they didn't, they would be thrown into the fire. There were three men who didn't bow down to him and got thrown into the fire because they would only serve their God. The king couldn't believe his eyes when he looked into the fire to see not three but four guys in the fire—the fourth looking like the Son of God. When they came out of the fire, they were not burned and didn't even smell like smoke.

There are many days when I reflect on my childhood and feel as if I walked through the fire and didn't get burned or consumed by the flames. I walked away feeling as though I didn't even smell like smoke. I have encountered so many people struggling with battles beyond their strength—their identity was wrapped up in victimhood, and they had lost themselves. They lost their motivation and strength, their fire, and their passion. I understand how hard it is to go through these unimaginable trials, but I was the only one who could change the outcome of my life despite how it started. No one else could do that for me. It's a personal decision that I have had to make every day.

My faith was tested, and I learned so much from that. I learned the balance between loving your neighbor and honoring your parents while still having healthy boundaries in place. I learned how to have grace for those who have hurt me. I gained an understanding of my parents' childhood and past to learn how that affected the choices they made.

When it came to reflecting on the way that I was raised, I made a decision to process my parents' upbringing. My upbringing directly reflects the decisions I make, and I knew that was true for them, too.

My dad's dad died when he was three, and his mom was a drug dealer. At a young age, she would strap him with drugs and send him down the street to sell them for her. He grew up without a role model and was using street drugs. This trickled into the teenage years, and that got him mixed into the wrong crowds in school. As I learned more about the home he was raised in, it made sense that we were raised in a similar home. This does not mean I deemed his actions right, but often, these patterns repeat themselves, which led me to have a greater understanding of their decisions.

My mom's mom raised her and her two sisters by herself, each having a different dad. My mom's dad left when she was only two and didn't have contact with her until she was eighteen years old. She lost contact with him for many years until she found her stepsister. My mom greatly struggled with not having a father figure, which led her to fight hard for us to have one. Consequently, she stayed with my dad when she should have left.

Our parents didn't get married until I was eight or nine. Their union took place in our family's living room. I remember sitting on the couch as they stood in front of the fireplace making promises I wasn't sure they could keep. The phone rang, and it felt awkward in the room, but people laughed. This was my first look into what marriage was.

My parents have always had an on-and-off relationship. They loved each other, but my dad made it hard with his addiction to keep our home safe. My mom wrestled with that as she wanted what was best for us kids. Both my mom and dad's childhood crept into their marriage and the way that they raised us kids.

When we're able to understand someone's upbringing, it helps us to see through the lens of their decisions. I often look at the decisions that I have made and continue to make, and I see a direct correlation to how I was raised. I often can't sit still for very long. I hate jobs that aren't flexible, and I get bored very easily. I constantly need affirmations that I didn't get as a child. I know this comes from living a life of chaos where nothing was ever consistent. In school, I would get special treatment since all my teachers knew about what was going on at home, so I didn't always have to go to class. My floral teacher would let me do independent study, and I would just go sit in the greenhouse for an hour every day. The lunchroom was so scary to me, so I would go get a pass and sit in the library. I was so accustomed to hiding by that point. I was used to having to lie, to hide things, and it made me uncomfortable to look people in the eyes. At the same time, I didn't want to be alone.

Growing up, I did everything I could to just get through each day, which often looked like avoiding certain places and people. When something would trigger my emotions, I would just ask my teacher if I could leave. Most of the time, they were happy to let me go to the library to go clear my head.

I'm grateful that these times in our lives aren't places we stay but rather places that we're passing through. Although I still struggle with these responses to my emotions, these are things that I am now aware I am doing. When we have awareness of our emotional responses, then we're able to acknowledge and work on them. When I know that I'm having a rough day, I will make sure I don't isolate myself from people. If I'm feeling stressed, I'll make a cup of tea and grab a book instead of sleeping it off. I have spent a lot of time reflecting on my habits and what triggers me to help find freedom from them. I can continue to work on these by having grace for myself knowing just how far I have come.

As much as my faith has carried me to this point, so has my community. My church has carried the weight with me and has continued to rejoice with me. Having a Godly community changes everything. The thing I see often with people coming from broken homes and remaining broken is a lack of community. We were never meant to do this life alone, and what's worse than doing it alone is doing it with the wrong people:

> The people who will hand the alcoholic a beer.

> The person who tells you to get over it but has no idea what you're going through.

> The one who doesn't care about you but just wants to know all your dirty secrets.

One of the best things I did was surround myself with people who I wanted to emulate. I spent time with married couples who were living a Godly marriage. I gathered with people who regularly attended Bible study with me. I found ladies in the church that were ready to go to every Bible study and church event within a thirty-mile radius of my hometown.

I was doing something almost every night of the week. Tuesday was prayer, Wednesday night was youth group, and Friday was a women's Bible study. I'd get there early to enjoy a hot peach tea and clean the house. It was a special time preparing a place where ministry was flowing from.

Friday night, we'd go to a worship service, and Saturday, we'd go to another service. Come Sunday morning, I would sit for two services at my home church and listen to the same message twice. I would find that after listening to it twice, I'd learn more the second time. I loved to worship. I would take a group of youth students on Wednesday night to a worship service at North Central University. We'd go from 10 p.m. until midnight, and on the way home, we'd often stop for breakfast. Some of my favorite nights were the ones I spent all hours of the night praising God. I had so much to praise him for.

One time, I went to a marriage conference, single at seventeen. I deeply desired to be married, so I put myself in a room full of married people desiring to learn more about each other and how to heal from their childhoods. I thought to myself, "Well, it's probably better to do this now before I'm married than to wait and do this later." It was awkward and hard to be in this room; I didn't feel like I belonged.

However, I often wonder what divorce rates would look like if single people put themselves in these rooms more often and made themselves whole instead of trying to find someone to make them whole. What if young people took a look in the mirror and took time to find healing instead of looking at social media to tell them what healing looks like? Healing isn't a vacation at the beach, as nice as that sounds. Healing isn't a weekend out on the town to forget about your ex. Healing is found in your room, alone with your messy self and Jesus. Healing is found with your church family speaking life over you. Healing is found when you're at the end of yourself and you desperately need Jesus. Decide how you want your life to look, and do whatever it takes to get there. It may be in small subtle ways, or it could be a choice that you make today that you've been waiting months or years to make. I can look back on the little decisions and the large ones, and despite how terrifying it was to make them, I'm grateful that I did.

※ ※ ※

As my junior year came to an end, my floral class took a field trip to a technical college in the cities that had a Floral Design program. We got to take a look into the classroom and storefront that they occupied. Towards the end of the tour, the teacher announced to our class that next year would be the last year that they would have this program. All the other colleges had closed their programs, and this school was the last one to have it. I felt so many emotions wash over me, "How can this be? This is the one degree that I want to pursue." I rushed over to the professor as the class was getting ready to head out. I asked, "Is there any way that I could go through this program as a senior in high school?" She replied, "Absolutely if you get approved for PSEO, you're able to go through the program." I was thrilled and terrified all at the same time. I knew that my academics were not where they needed to be for me to be able to do PSEO. I was already doing the bare minimum to be able to just graduate. You needed to be in the top 2/3 of your class, and I was not even close.

We got back to school, and I set up a meeting with my guidance counselor. I went over my academics and applied for an appeal to do PSEO. We talked through the plan and my heart behind wanting to do this. With a smile on her face, they approved it, but... I would have to attend summer school. I felt so grateful that I had the opportunity to almost start over with a new school and new friends. I was so grateful I asked.

Summer school started, and shockingly, I was the only student who didn't have to be there. It was only for six weeks for a few hours every day. The rowdy kids made it very hard to focus on the work that they gave me, so the teacher gave me my own little office. I did so well that they let me out a week early. I was happy to be able to enjoy a little bit of summer before I started my exciting new journey at college. This was huge for me because I was about to become the first person in my family to graduate high school, let alone go to college.

My senior year of high school quickly came to be. After the last three years of designing flowers in high school and working part-time at the local grocery store as a floral clerk, deciding I'd pursue a degree in floral design was the best thing for me. I loved everything about not having normal classes, or even having to step foot back into high school. Part of me was sad to miss certain days, but it truly was everything I needed.

At college, we had a small class of twelve people, and each student was at least ten years older than me.

I felt like I was cheating most days because a lot of the instructions were about things that I learned in my high school floral classes. This opportunity gave me the much-needed freedom that I desired. There were so many moments where I just paused and felt so grateful.

As Thanksgiving approached, I talked to my dad for the first time in three years. It wasn't legal for us to talk, so we had to be careful that he wouldn't get in trouble. We put in an appeal to get the no-contact order dismissed so that we could spend Christmas together. In the ten days leading up to Christmas, my friend asked me to go with her to Hawaii to visit her family. It was going to cost over $1,000 for me to go, and I knew that I didn't have the money. I knew I had to call my dad, and I felt he would be receptive to giving me the money. Let's just say he had a lot of making up to do.

But I was nervous to ask anything from him. One time, we went to an outdoors store—he loved the outdoors and fishing—and I ended up seeing this vest that I wanted very badly. I asked and asked again, and he told me that we'd come back to get it. I knew that was a straight up lie and he was avoiding the situation. It was one hundred dollars, so I understood that it could be a lot for an unplanned purchase, but he was also the same guy who would put a one-hundred-dollar bill under my pillow from the tooth fairy. He truly did it to himself; he taught us that money was never an issue when it's always been the issue. Most kids would get maybe a dollar when they lost a tooth; a hundred dollars made me feel like we weren't poor even though we were.

In the end, I convinced him to buy the vest for me. With this in mind, I called him and reasoned with him. I was the only child in our family that was graduating high school, let alone taking college classes at the same time. All I wanted was to get away for ten days during my senior year of high school.

It worked.

He told me how proud he was of me and agreed to pay for it. I was so grateful, and I was looking forward to this being the start of us rebuilding our relationship. I was nervous but tried not to get my hopes up this time. My dad often let me down, which made it hard to believe that he was actually going to pay for my trip until I had the money in hand.

He delivered.

* * *

I remember taking my very first plane ride out of the Minneapolis airport. We woke up that morning extra early only to realize my friend's mom forgot her ID. What a way to start this trip, but it all worked out. It was a bumpy take off as the gloomy clouds filled the little round windows and raindrops dripped off of them. I almost threw up while we were still going up into the gray clouds that filled the sky, and I was not looking forward to the additional five hours of flying over the ocean once we got to LA.

Once we got to Kona and watched the sunset, I remember this gratefulness for my dad—this love and compassion and forgiveness towards him. As rough as my life often was with him, these were moments of healing and hope for what was to come in our relationship. For the first time in many years, I felt as though I finally had my dad back.

We had an incredible trip snorkeling and visiting the beaches and waterfalls. When I returned home on Christmas Eve, I got to my aunt's house to see my dad legally for the first time in three years. Nervously, I wanted to show my dad what I bought with his money, but I told myself I wouldn't tell him until I saw him. I lifted the side of my shirt to my rib cage where I had gotten a tattoo on one of our dog's paws. Although he's covered in tattoos, he made it very clear he didn't want us girls to have any. After he cooled down, he admitted he loved it. In Hawaii, you don't have to be eighteen or have a parent's permission to get a tattoo.

Although I wasn't living at home, we enjoyed Christmas together as a family once again. I remember feeling so grateful for the trip and this new relationship with my dad. He looked great and was sober. After Christmas, he'd often pick me up from college to spend time with me. I'd get in the car, and he'd often want to take home whatever project I made. He was such a blast to be around, always having a story to tell. I'd get in the car, and "Hotel California" would be on the radio, and he'd be singing his heart out.

One day, I was heading home from college when I was driving down the highway and I was sideswiped by a semi. Thankfully, I was physically okay, but I was an emotional mess. The semi didn't stop, and I ended up hitting a truck. I called my dad bawling, and he came to get me. I so badly wanted him to just be with me because I was scared. This was new for me as I was used to being afraid of him. I loved having him back; this wasn't something I ever thought I'd have. For years, I desperately just wanted my dad in my life. There was still something inside of me that just wanted my dad when something happened. I think I cried even harder, not for being scared but to be able to pick up my phone and call him, knowing that he was going to be there.

CHAPTER 14

MY WORST NIGHTMARE

It had been almost a month of having him present in my life, and he started moving things back home. He was rekindling his relationship with my mom after years of being separated. He got to meet the guy that I was dating and it was honestly so nice for him to enter into that part of my life. One night I stopped by my mom's house to grab something. I was sitting at a desk in my childhood bedroom when my dad came in and told me that they were moving his bike to the shop. He made some sort of comment about something he was selling, and I joked about what he could buy me with the money he'd made from it. He gave me a big hug and kiss and he headed out the door.

A couple of days went by, and I was running some errands, getting ready for a busy Valentine's weekend at the floral shop. I went out to coffee with an old friend, and a couple from my church bought me coffee. It was a sweet little coffee shop and was my favorite place to visit. It was placed on the corner of the main street in town and had the coziest and most charming vibe. I had friends that worked there, and they made my coffee with extra love. I'm convinced this is true because it always tasted better when they made it. I think what I loved the most about this place was the people. I would just sit in there, and throughout the day, I'd see just about the whole congregation come through.

I texted my dad when I got my coffee and headed to my mom's house to get ready before I went to a hockey game. I was in her bathroom curling my hair when I heard the uncontrollable cries of my mom coming from the outside deck. My heart dropped— this wasn't just any cry. I stepped out of the bathroom, and as I rounded the corner, my eyes met her friend that was sitting on the couch. She immediately stepped into my path and grabbed my shoulders. The words spilled out of my mouth easily: "My dad's dead, isn't he?"

She burst into tears, shaking her head, and I met my mom on the deck with a hug. I immediately hopped into my car and started driving to my boyfriend's house. I called him, confused, and told him, "I think my dad died." I kept saying "I think" because I didn't know. I didn't see the body or have any confirmation. I went to his house and sat in the living room with his parents. They were the family that I never got to have. His parents did so much for me. From the countless dinners to the hugs from his mom, they supported me in the hardest nights and the longest days.

My mom's friend went to check on my dad when my mom couldn't get ahold of him. My brother was already in the hospital for a drug overdose, and my sister was in Texas on vacation with my aunts. I went to the hockey game in complete shock. I couldn't get myself to call my sister, which I regretted because she found out on social media after one of my brother's friends posted about it. We talked for a while until she could get to the nearest airport, which was hours away. She didn't blame me as I was in complete shock. I had never lost someone so close to me.

The following weeks were hell, trying to get the truth of what happened. My mom wouldn't let us see the body, and it took months to plan the funeral. My church family surrounded me and held me up during this difficult time.

My worst nightmare came true when I learned that I lost my dad to a heroin overdose.

Nothing prepares you for the death of a parent, especially one that wasn't around for very long. You almost grieve the loss of the person and the loss of the relationship you never got to have. It was three months shy of my high school and college graduation, and six months from my eighteenth birthday. It was devastating to come to grips with how much he was going to miss out on...

At his funeral, we gathered our close family and friends. People smoked cigars around his custom motorcycle that he made. I remember wearing this maroon dress that was four inches too short. I looked like I was about to go to a club, but I honestly didn't care. I just needed to find something to wear that I could throw away afterward. I went to the bathroom and chugged mini bottles of liquor with my sister before I said a few words out of my brown leather notebook in the best way that I could.

> *Dad,*
>
> *I can't even begin to put into words how I feel. It hurts to know that you won't be at my high school or college graduation in a few months. You won't be there for my eighteenth birthday or when I walk down the aisle one day. I loved your passion for people and that you were always a badass. No one messed with you. I'm sorry for the people that did you wrong. I hope they get what they deserve because you didn't deserve what you went through.*
>
> *Your Little Girl*

As I sat and listened to this pastor, I heard words that I prayed for but never knew I'd hear. I learned that my father made a personal decision to follow Jesus—that he was saved and served faithfully in the local church in the sound booth. The Pastor talked about how loved he was and how he served everything that he could.

THIS. CHANGED. EVERYTHING.

Knowing that my dad was in Heaven, fully healed, and in perfect peace with Jesus changed the way I grieve. Yes, it's still hard, but it brings joy to the deepest part of me. Over the three years he wasn't in my life, God was moving and at work in his heart. As much as I wanted to regret those years of him not being around, I couldn't because our absence from his life led him to repentance.

One of the things I struggled with for many years was not seeing his body. It was hard not to wonder if he went into hiding again, and the possibility that this time, he didn't take us with him. He always said that if we ever went back into hiding, he'd never take us with him. Every part of me didn't want to believe he overdosed. My dad's house was also missing things that he would have taken with him, and a lot didn't make sense in the days after his death.

I thought maybe someone had given him a 'hotshot'—that's when someone injects you with a deadly drug to make it look like an overdose. Many CIs have died this way, making it look like they did it to themselves. Or if his death was from the week before when my brother was in the ICU from a bad batch of heroin and my dad kicked down a drug dealer's door. I wanted to believe anything but him doing it to himself. What made it harder was when we got the police report, it said that my brother had died and not my dad. My brother was alive and in the hospital due to a drug overdose that happened a few days prior. They both have the same name, although my brother is Jr, and they have a massive age gap.

I was a mess, but I did what I needed to do to get ready for graduation. I picked out a dress and prepared for a week of mixed emotions. In the mess of my emotions, I sat down in a salon chair and asked the hairdresser to chop off my long, beautiful hair. As the shears gilded across my hair, I burst into tears. Sobbing and speechless, the hairdresser whipped my chair around.

"What is your problem? You asked for this."

I was crying even harder as I tried to get the words out. "You don't understand. My dad died, and I'm walking across the stage tomorrow at graduation."

The hairdresser was horrified that she responded in the way she did. I didn't mean to upset her. It wasn't because of her that I was crying. My dad loved my long hair, and, in spite, I chopped it all off. I felt like in my rebellion maybe it would bring him back. Maybe if I got myself in enough trouble, he'd come back and check up on me.

The truth was, I was desperate. I just wanted to be held.

My whole family came to watch me walk across the stage at my college graduation. The day was surrounded by family as I wore my cap adorned with an orchard crown. Floral school was the best thing that happened to me that year.

A few weeks later, I was to walk across the stage of my high school graduation. Ironically, I had more anxiety about my high school graduation than my college one. I had been so removed from everyone in high school for the nine months I was attending college that I felt more out of place with my high school peers.

On the morning of my high school graduation, I got in my car and started driving up north. I decided I couldn't do it. It was way too hard. I took away the tickets from my mom and brother because he was way too messed up to come, and someone needed to stay home to watch him. As I headed north to the North Shore, a friend called me. He reached out and encouraged me to finish what I started. So, I did just that. I turned my car around and got ready for the afternoon. I walked across that stage to get the thing that I fought many battles behind closed doors to get—countless tears, many homes, and sleepless nights. Many people watched and waited for this day. Teachers and friends encouraged me along the way.

The summer after graduation, I fell into a spree of going out to parties, although I was living with a pastor's family that took me in. I thought for sure that would help me stay levelheaded. The warm Minnesota summers just have something in the air that causes you to be down for a good time. Country music blaring with the windows down always seemed to pair nicely with a bonfire and a few cold ones. I'd go to a party here and there. It was enjoyable to be able to feel my age for once.

I vividly recall sitting at a local coffee shop when a dear friend of mine walked in. He sat with me for a while and talked until another young man walked in. It was a guy from my third-grade class that he also happened to know, so we all sat and talked for hours. It was the week leading up to my eighteenth birthday, and I had my name in the books at a tattoo shop that did all my dad's tattoos. As we chatted, I asked them their thoughts, and they thought for sure a leg tattoo was the way to go. So, August 5th rolled around, and I walked into this tattoo shop, shaking in my boots. This place used to have gang members hanging around it, and being Hollywood's daughter, it always made me nervous that someone might know who I was. I hopped on the chair and told the tattoo artist I wanted a thigh full of flowers, and he did just that. And I still love it.

That night, I went out, and that led me to go to several parties that weekend. I met some people from the town over, and they seemed to have the partying thing down. There was always another one planned for the next night. I went to three parties that weekend. Often, when I'd go to parties, people who knew me would give me this "look"—the look that I shouldn't be there or a shocked look. They knew I was living with a local pastor's family, and my drunk conversations were mostly around Jesus. I think I enjoyed being taken care of while I laid on the floor drunk—finally, I was the one being taken care of rather than the other way around.

There was one party that I went to where one of the guys that was a few years older than me had parents who hung around the same gang my dad was in. I tossed a few too many back, and a different guy was preying on me. The guy that knew me asked me to come sit by him, and in the most understanding way you could talk to a drunk girl, he explained to me what the guy had been saying. He made sure that when I went to sleep that he stayed awake to be sure nothing happened. The next morning, he told me he knew my story. He knew everything I went through and stopped drinking to make sure I stayed safe. The truth was, I was drinking to cover up the pain of being eighteen and now fatherless.

Tatted and hungover, I stepped through the doors of my pastor's house. She looked up from the couch, and I knew instantly that she knew where I was. She saw my leg and asked where I'd been, but really, she knew and loved me anyway. She showed me grace when I didn't feel like I deserved it. She showed me Jesus in those moments that even though I was a sinner, he loved me anyway. I'm grateful for those in my life who show me the love of Jesus when I don't deserve it. That night, I started to pack my bags because I didn't feel worthy enough to live there.

She told me, "I want you here even more now."

I have never felt love like this before—love when I didn't want it, nor did I deserve it, and grace when I took the gift of their home for granted. Praise God for people who love you when loving you isn't easy. And she loved me despite the fact that I wasn't her child. She didn't have to love me; she chose to love me.

She was and still is full of wisdom and so was her momma. Her mom was the sweetest lady. When I was still in an unhealthy relationship, that woman looked me dead in the eyes and told me that I was never going to marry him. The relationship ended soon after. As my heart became more and more on fire for Jesus, I wanted his best for my life, not mine. I wanted to walk in the fullness of what he had for me no matter what that looked like.

That fall, I enrolled in a community college to further my education. A few weeks in, I was a mess missing my dad and school wasn't it for me. I could feel that I needed to do something else. After being told it was going to cost me five thousand dollars to withdraw from college, my counselor slipped a note under the dean's door, and two hours later, I was removed from the school. It was wiped off my record like I never even enrolled, and they let me return my books for a full refund. That, my friend, is called a favor.

Not too long after I dropped out of college, the grocery store where I used to work as a floral clerk called and asked for my help. They asked me if I'd be willing to work at their location forty-five minutes east of my hometown. I said yes to designing for them. The downfall to accepting this position was the long commute every day. Still, it was such a relief to continue to pursue my passion for floral design. Designing was so helpful to the grief that I was walking through.

A few weeks into working there, I got to know the lady who oversaw all of the floral departments in the company. At that time, we didn't have a manager, and she extended an offer to me. I became the youngest department manager, overseeing six employees who were all older than me. As hard as it was, it taught me that, this too, I was able to overcome. I was entrusted with a role with great responsibility, and I thrived in it. Working hard was never something that I lacked—it's always been something I enjoyed.

As small of a person as I am (all 4'11 of me), the Lord has given me boldness and courage. I am not afraid to speak my mind and do the right thing, no matter how hard it is. I was despised for my age, but that was never tolerated in my department. One employee would constantly make comments about my age, and countless times he went to management with the lack of faith he had in me to do my job. It ultimately led to him getting fired. If my childhood showed me anything, it was to stand up for myself and for what is right.

One day, I noticed this young pretty girl who was picking out some roses. She was buying quite a few of them, and the way she carried herself resonated with me. It was how I was currently carrying myself. There was a longing in her eyes.

I said to her, "Do you mind if I help you bring these to your car?"

Her face lit up, and she said, "I would really appreciate that"

I carried them to her car, and the words just slipped out of my mouth. "Are you okay?"

Tears filled her eyes.

"My mom passed away several years ago in a car accident, and I'm on my way to the cemetery."

I embraced her with a big hug and told her how I was struggling with the recent death of my father. We talked and exchanged numbers. I kept in contact for a few years and later found out that she was also a believer.

This job was many things for me, but in the end, it was a place I was just passing through. A little over a year later, I returned to my sweet little hometown, and I moved back in with the pastor's family. I picked up where I left off at the breakfast place as a server. During the holidays, I would help at the local flower shop, arranging the most beautiful arrangements. I really enjoyed this season of being home. As we neared the summer, I was offered a role that I never expected. My youth pastor asked me if I would be an intern for the summer. I felt so unworthy of this. Having been in two ungodly dating relationships and a few parties later, I surely shouldn't have been entrusted with leading and having influence on the next generation. Despite my feelings, I said yes.

That summer was filled with relationships, reading, and getting to know God in a deeper way. It allowed me to have fun and love on the students. In this season, I valued myself in a way I didn't before. I equipped myself to be the best woman that I could be, and it got me thinking about how to position myself to one day be a wife. I longed to be a wife. I got a journal and started journaling to my future husband.

Although I was pursuing all things that were good, I couldn't help but get a special tattoo in honor of my dad. During the time we weren't legally able to speak to each other, we'd often leave little note writing back and forth in my grandma's cupboard. It was the only way we could communicate. After he passed away, I went to her house and found the tiny little yellow Post-It note in the spice cupboard.

"I love u to - papa."

Those five words meant everything to me to read. I took that Post-It note to a tattoo shop to get it engraved into my wrist. I didn't even care about his misspelled use of 'to.' I wanted it tattooed exactly as he wrote it—a simple reminder of a father's love. I knew that I could take that wherever I would go.

As that summer was coming to an end, I left like God was calling me to a place I have never been. I applied to many colleges and a missionary school.

I was denied my college choice and got accepted to a missionary school in Nicaragua. So, I planned on packing my bags and heading there that fall. Towards the middle of summer, the peace protest got worse in Nicaragua, and I felt like the Lord was leading me in a different way.

CHAPTER 15

A SIMPLE PRAYER

There was a customer that I had at the little breakfast place where I worked at when I was fifteen. He'd come in often and I even started seeing him at Tuesday prayer and church events. He was an older gentleman that lost his wife a few years earlier. I loved seeing him come through the front doors of the restaurant. He was a light to so many. Our conversations were never long due to the mad rush of churchgoers coming in for brunch, but he always let me know that he was praying for me. He'd text me and leave me messages on social media often. He'd call, and if I didn't answer, he'd leave me a voicemail to let me know that he was praying for me.

I once went to get a tour of his house and the landing strip in his field that his son uses when he's out flying his airplane. We hopped into his antique

truck and drove around this little farm. We'd talk
about his wife and the legacy that she left. He'd talk
about his lunches at Applebee's and the waitresses he
has built relationships with. He did ministry everywhere he went—and I mean everywhere. He didn't
care about what a person thought, he shared Jesus
with them and let them know that he was praying
for them.

I honestly can say that I believe that's part of
how I've gotten to where I am, through his prayers
and many others. I knew that no matter where I was,
someone was praying on my behalf. Ever since having
left for college, and even now that I am married, I still
will get a call every so often. I look forward to those
calls because I don't know how many that I have left.

PART II
Hopeful

CHAPTER 16

A PLACE YOU'VE NEVER BEEN BEFORE

These words kept being laid on my heart, over and over again. Surely, I hadn't been to a lot of places, and I was convinced I was going to be a missionary. I was in prayer constantly waiting for a revelation of what that meant for me.

It was Father's Day weekend, and it hit me. I was sitting on the couch and remembered that one of the families that had taken me in was about to bring their youngest son to college in a few weeks. He was heading to South Florida to a Christian college. Their son and I had a very close relationship, so I asked him if it would be weird for me to apply. Of course, he wasn't weirded out but was excited that there was even a chance I could go with him. Every private college I applied to, I was denied because of my academics. I even sent letters with my application because I was just a girl trying to get out of my house alive and I didn't think that my past should hold me back from future opportunities. I didn't want to get my hopes up, and I applied just to see what would happen.

I talked and prayed with his mom. She was thrilled I even applied. That weekend being my dad's birthday and Father's Day was always hard for me. This year, however, it gave me a spur of strength to look at what was ahead of me.

I was driving when I got the call and had to pull over. To my complete surprise, I got a call that I was accepted. I shrieked with excitement and absolute fear. I had chills all over my body.

I couldn't believe it.

I quickly called the family whose son was going, and they were thrilled. I had less than two weeks to pack up my whole life to move to a place I have never been to and a college I have never heard of. I put my notice in at the breakfast place where I had been working, where I was managing the front of house staff. Summer camp was the following week, and I started wrapping up my internship. As I was getting my heart ready to leave, I kept feeling like this year would be the year I was going to meet my husband. I never was one to voice things like this, but I really felt like that was what the Lord had for me, so I was believing in it.

This experience was going to be so different for me. Although I attended community college while in high school to get my floral degree, this was a four-year program that would allow me to have the total college experience I so desperately wanted. From living in the dorms to meeting college friends, I was looking forward to all of it—to starting over.

I had to share the news with my sister, and that left us both emotional. I went to Build-a-Bear and got a bunny that held a surfboard with a little voice recording of me telling her how much I loved her. After nineteen years of living in the same state as each other, it was the first time I'd be living so far away from her. I knew that I was going to miss our coffee dates and dinners, our pedicures and Mexican lunch dates. I was going to miss everything about living near her.

The two weeks flew by as I went through and packed up my belongings. I remember meeting my ex-boyfriend to give him his old hockey sweatshirts back over a year and a half after we broke up, and his reaction to me leaving was closure. I know it was petty of me to do that, but I couldn't donate them. There was such joy and peace as I shared that I was heading to Florida to go to school for ministry. That wasn't the girl he dated, and it felt good that the old ways were gone. This interaction was many things. The toxic cycle was over, and this new way was better. I'm grateful for those three years that we dated despite how messy it was. He and his family were exactly what I needed in that season. Especially after losing my dad, I wasn't able to make any big life decisions—I just wanted to stay busy. I was depressed and I know I was emotionally a lot to handle. But I was grateful for those whose lives impacted mine despite how things ended.

It is amazing to me how we can become new, whole people in Christ.

* * *

The second week of August came around, and we packed up the truck. The son had to leave some things behind because I literally packed my whole life. I'm grateful for our relationship and the way his face lit up when he talked about his sister coming to college with him. He was a brother that I've always wanted, and our friendship was life-giving. Girls would often be jealous of our friendship because we were so used to doing life together.

We drove many hours down to South Florida, and when we made it, I was nervous and excited. His mom was over the moon for us to experience it together. We drove past our campus and over the bridge to Palm Beach Island. I remember standing along the ocean, looking out and being reminded of God's faithfulness in my life. Earlier that spring, I wanted a one-week beachfront vacation but started my internship instead. Now I had an opportunity for a four-year beach destination.

We headed to campus to get settled into our dorms. I was so overjoyed to be getting a college experience—this was something that I never expected to get. His mom helped me pick out decor and collect my school supplies. We went to the opening rally, and I had goosebumps. The ceremony moved me to tears, and I knew at that moment, I was exactly where I was supposed to be. I was registered in the School of Ministry to start my degree plan for Pastoral Care and Counseling. My heart was to share biblical truth and guide people to find freedom and healing. Soon classes would start, and his parents got packed up to head back home.

A few weeks into college I started experiencing a really painful toothache. This toothache turned into a 3 a.m.Uber ride to the emergency room because the pain was unbearable. I was sent home with pain meds, and I found a friend to drive me to the dentist the next morning. I found out that my tooth broke, and I had a severe infection. I ended up having the tooth pulled, and I was given stitches.

One thing about me and my sister is that we have passed out from blood and needles since we were the age of five. This time, I was passed out for longer, and they started yelling code something. I jolted awake and I saw them putting a little thing under my nose— some sort of smelly thing to make me wake up. I learned later these were smelling salts, often given to patients who pass out. It worked rather well, and they sent me on my way back to my dorm. A month into school, I had already been down and out for a week recovering. I had the sweetest pottery teacher that would make me smoothies and take them to me. I felt so weak and defeated, and this made it so much more bearable.

Soon, I was back on my feet. Living in South Florida had already been so healing for me. The walks to the beach and the daily visits to local coffee shops were so restful for me. I colored my hair bleach blonde, and my skin was sun-kissed. This new life was good to me. For once, I felt "normal." I was meeting so many new students, most of them knowing me as the girl who came with her little brother to college, and I'd smile and say, "Yep, that's me."

The plan was that at the end of this year I would transfer to a Christian college in Minneapolis, which was my first pick. It was fun to know that I was just passing through this beautiful place. Life on campus was fun, but so was exploring off-campus. I would often grab my longboard and skate to a beach shack to get an Acai bowl a few blocks from campus, or I'd go to get an iced lavender latte in the city square.

I met a few guys that quickly became close friends. We would spend time longboarding, and I would listen to stories about all these boy-crazy girls. One day, I was sitting outside of the café when a guy approached me with a german shepherd. We talked for a while as I pet his dog. I learned that he was a recovering alcoholic. Because of my past, I had no judgment, but I thought it was odd how open he was.

He started messaging me, and his messages became more and more frequent. Then he started showing up everywhere I was, which made me uncomfortable and annoyed. He was a bigger-built guy and was in the business program but lived off campus. He kept asking me on a date to the restaurant where he worked and later made a comment that he'd only have one glass of wine. A huge red flag went off. If he was a recovering alcoholic, then why would he be okay with a drink? I didn't even want to go on a date in the first place, and I definitely didn't want to go now.

I was working at a flower shop as a floral designer on the historic Worth Avenue on the island of Palm Beach. This place was so small and quaint. I loved it. I made it known to my boss about this guy, and one day he stopped into the shop. It was so uncomfortable, and she could even tell that something was off. I proceeded to text this guy that I was uncomfortable and that he needed to leave me alone. That's when it all blew up.

He proceeded to sit outside my dorm building. He'd call and place orders at my work. He would park outside my work and, eventually, he got a job in the school café—the only place I could use my meal plan on campus. I'd see him on my walks and in the local town square. This man was everywhere and wouldn't leave me alone.

I started going to a counselor at the school to let them know what was going on. After many known attempts to ask him to leave me alone, he was still following and watching me. One day, I went to the chapel and sat in the front row, and he came and sat next to me. I got up and ran out as fast as I could only to have him chase after me. I yelled, "Leave me the hell alone" as loud as I could in the middle of the day on my crowded college campus. That got everyone's attention.

I went to the Dean of the School of Ministry to let him know what was going on and how it was affecting me academically. As I was sharing this, I could see a look wash over him that made me even more concerned. You could see the compassion in his eyes. He reached for his cell phone and told me that we had to leave right now.

He proceeded to tell me, "I had a young man come to talk to me to get more involved with the ministry department. And he also said, "There's this girl, and when God brings us together, then she'll be my girlfriend." With fear in his eyes he said, "I so badly wanted to know who this girl was because I was concerned for her safety."

Tears rolled down my face as this was the first time I felt heard and seen over the past several weeks. My fears were not just mine but also someone with great influence at the college. After many long conversations and meetings, I filed for a Title IX. A Title IX is something that you can file for when you've been sexually harassed, and it is put in place to protect college students in this situation.

It felt weird to have my feelings and fears

validated by somebody at the university that had a personal experience with this threatening man. The few weeks of investigating felt never-ending. The young man continued to follow me and watch me without my knowledge. Campus safety would bring me to and from classes and at times ate lunch with me. They invited me to come back to the security room when they found footage of him following and watching me. We had the evidence we needed.

The day came when they made a decision. I was terrified to find out what else they had found out. I walked into this room where a member of the university staff met me. She passed a nicely folded piece of paper over and explained to me that they kicked him out of the university and banned him from campus. Tears streamed down my face. It hit me that I wasn't exaggerating. Throughout this whole process, every part of me wanted to drop it because it wasn't as bad as some things that I had gone through, and I just felt like I should just get over it. I'm grateful that I didn't and that I stood my ground. She thanked me for stepping up right away because many college-aged girls would have kept quiet and either something bad would have happened or years later, they would wish that they had spoken up.

Before that meeting ended, I had already texted my sister to book my flight home. Our plan was that if he was getting kicked out, that I would take the next flight home out of Florida to let a few weeks go by for everything to calm down. I remember sitting at the airport reflecting on the goodness of God. He was my protector in that season—his handprint was all over it. I knew that he was fighting for me.

It was a relief to be home. I was finally able to rest my mind and process what had happened so far. Between getting sick and being stalked, it had been a really rough year. I wanted nothing more than to just stay home and not go back to school. While I was home, I stayed with a family that I spent the last three years living with before I moved for college. Its "home" to me. The mom is a pastor at the church that I attended, she's my spiritual momma and her husband has been a dad to me. They both gave me the 'look' when I sat on their bed crying that I don't want to go back—the look that a loving father gives to his daughter that means: *You got this and you're going back.*

He looked at me and said, "Did you find your prince charming yet?"

Obviously, I hadn't, or this guy would be long gone.

He proceeded to say, "If you don't go back, you may miss the opportunity. If you know that God brought you all the way down there, shouldn't you wait to find out why?"

There was so much wisdom in that sentence that I greatly lacked in those moments. I was operating out of fear and pure emotions when I needed to rest on what the Lord was asking and requiring of me in this season. With renewed strength, I headed back to South Florida.

As hard as it was to walk through that, it resurfaced a lot of things from my past that I hadn't had to worry about for some time. When we were in hiding, we always watched our surroundings. That never left me. I felt like I was right back to that same level of worry and fear, except this time, I was by myself. I'm grateful for the ability to adapt to new ways of life rather quickly. The Lord evidently gave me the strength to endure this season.

As the school year came to an end, I was really disappointed with how I did. I got three total college credits for $30,000. I had to drop out of classes and failed a few trying to just apply myself even when I couldn't show up. If you ask me, that was not a good deal.

CHAPTER 17

THANK YOU, JESUS

With three weeks left until my one-way flight back to
Minnesota, something didn't feel right. I still didn't
understand why God called me to Florida in the first
place. I know sometimes we don't see the significance
in a season right away or until many years later, but
this one was different.

Coming to Florida, I really felt like I was going to
meet the love of my life. I was praying daily for years
for him. I was intentionally journaling for him and
patiently waiting. And let me tell you, I did not meet
anyone at school that was the right candidate. My
college campus was large, and there were a lot of nice
guys, but they were just nice guys that grew up going
to church. Many of them were simply living for the
world. It was a beautiful campus less than a mile from
the ocean. I get how easy it would be to go to school
there just for the view.

I got a call from a lady that my professor went to church with and introduced me to. We met a few times and prayed together. She was a sweet friend to have that was older and settled down in life. I met with her one last time before things got busy with moving home.

She asked me, "Do you think that you saw and experienced what God has brought you here for? I don't think you have, and I don't think you should go home yet."

We continued to walk down historic Worth Avenue as I processed those words. Dumbfounded, I stopped and said, "I know that I haven't."

At that moment, I knew that despite my every desire to go home, I had to stay. My boss at the Florida flower shop was thrilled to keep me because she was sad to see me go. She helped me find the sweetest little mother-in-law suite where I could live off-campus. I didn't have a car, so I bought a small green moped that I named 'The Green Bean.' It got me to and from work on the island. Throughout this process, I made a promise to God that I'd give him one more year here—just one more year to see why I was there. I was all alone in the city that he brought me to—school was out and all my friends went home. Now it was just me on my own, living in the same city as my stalker. That alone took crazy faith to trust that I was still walking in his will for my life.

Easter Sunday rolled around, and I went to the

church that I had been attending on and off since the fall. I knew that with me staying, I really needed to be intentional about finding community. I had found this church in the most unexpected way. I was heading to the beach one Sunday morning when the beach was closed due to the red tide, so I decided to go to breakfast in the square.

On my way there, I saw the sign for the church located in the middle of the shopping square, and worship was about to start. I headed up the steps and sat in the back. Worship was about to begin, but I couldn't help but notice the couple in the front of the room that were distressed and crying. As much as I wanted to just stay in my seat and mind my own business, I couldn't help but go over and check on them. They proceeded to tell me that they were recovering addicts and her mom just passed away. They didn't have the money to fly home. Just as she finished telling me, someone from the church came to escort them out. I returned to my seat for worship, and I couldn't let it go. I knew I couldn't afford to pay for both of their flights. At that moment, the Lord laid on my heart just to pay for one of their flights.

I stepped out of my seat into the lobby and outside on the balcony where they took them. The staff was very confused as to why I was out there, but as we were talking, they told me that they can't just hand out money and that it would be a few days for them to get assistance. I told them that I would pay for one flight. Immediately after, a woman that was out there who served as a volunteer said she'd buy the other. I was shocked. I knew better than to give them money, so I booked the flights for them, and we arranged for a ride to the airport. Over the course of that hour, I was able to share my story and pray over them. I was blessed to be used by God to minister to this couple, even though it took the beach to be closed and my hunger to get me there.

I would meet that woman who paid for the other flight for coffee once in a while, and she would always make comments about the fact that I would never stay for service. I would normally sneak into the service for worship, and I would leave. I did this for months before I knew I was staying.

She invited me to join her for service on Easter Sunday and asked me to go out for coffee afterward. The coffee shop was located just below the theater that the church was in. Service ended, and we sat in the sun talking about where I wanted to serve and get involved. The pastor's wife and her daughter walked by and entered into small talk with the lady I was with. She introduced us and explained that I wanted to find a community. The other woman perked up and told me that there was a guy I needed to meet. She texted him and asked if we could wait to meet him once he was done with his Sunday role as the Location's Young Adults Pastor and Groups Coordinator.

I waited for what felt like forever.

Soon, this cute redheaded boy came around the corner. He had a muscular build and a perfect jawline. He was shy when she introduced him; his name was Austin. He was the young adults' pastor that oversaw that community downtown. Austin was quiet, and our exchange was quick, but I felt something. I felt it in the pit of my stomach. Bells went off in my head, and it hit me.

"I think I just found out why I'm here, I think I just met my husband."

These were the words that came out of my mouth to my pastor back home. She was thrilled and wanted all the details, even though at the time, I had none. I said there was a guy, and even though we only exchanged two words, I had never felt anything like I was feeling. We laughed and knew that I couldn't get ahead of myself. I just needed to wait and let the Lord do what he does best. Neither of us knew what that would look like, especially me. I just made a decision to stay. I was only two weeks into the year that I gave the Lord to show me, and he didn't make me wait long at all.

That next week, a friend of mine came to stay with me. I told her about Austin and she just shook her head in disbelief. Sunday morning came again, and I got to see him at church. I came back later that night for a night worship experience that they hosted. I asked a volunteer to get me signed up for their membership class and, of course, the cute redhead was the person handling the memberships. We talked for a few minutes, and he sent me an email. I almost died when I saw his last name was "Bouquet." I had been floral designing since I was fourteen, and I couldn't believe it. From what I felt on Easter Sunday to finding out his last name, I was taken aback.

Only the Lord, I thought over and over again.

That Thursday was a young adults' service. I invited my friend to join me, but she stayed home to have some quiet time to herself. She let me borrow her car, and I got there extremely early and offered to help set up. The cute redhead and I exchanged small talk, and a few girls were giving me looks and asking me far too many questions.

"Where are you from?"

"How do you know Austin?"

"What do you do for a living?"

"Are you single?"

I just shrugged them off because, well, I was distracted.

The night came to an end, and a different guy said that he could walk me to my car. I went to leave, and Austin cut this guy off and told him that he was actually walking me to the car. I was a little surprised but this made me feel better; I really didn't know the other guy. It was raining and he held my clear umbrella that oddly enough said "Love is in the air." We missed the road to my car, and we finally found it a block away. We talked a little bit, and he asked me to go to a putt putt golf course with him that upcoming weekend. I said yes, and we exchanged numbers and a time for him to pick me up.

I was excited and nervous for this group hangout. I had started over-analyzing this situation since I met this guy. At the time, my childhood best friend that I came to Florida with was sleeping on my couch and living with me for a few weeks before he was heading home. As a single woman and as a Christian, that didn't look good if you didn't know us or our story. He was a brother and forever will be.

The day came when we were going to grab dinner and play putt-putt with some young adults... or so I thought. He picked me up and took me out to a restaurant on the intercostal. We got there, and it was just us. We enjoyed a nice dinner, and he picked up the tab. It hit me that he didn't invite me to a young adult gathering; rather, this was a full-blown date. He never said that it was a young adult gathering. I just totally didn't think he'd ask me on a date. We continued the date at a putt-putt course, and I ended up beating him (or I like to think I did, anyway). After golf, he asked if I wanted to get a late Saturday night coffee as I so often did, or if I'd like a raincheck. We decided to hold off on the coffee, and before he dropped me off, we scheduled a date at the café a few days later.

I decided to take the membership class that I signed up for a few weeks prior. Of course, I'd be the girl in the room that went on a date with the teacher.

Our class ended, and he asked me to go get lunch with him. We got coffee that week, and before I left the coffee date, he already had another one planned. This experience was so different than any that I've ever had before. He never made me question or wonder if or when I'd see him again.

This was huge for me. A guy had never pursued me this way. I remember so many nights that previously were filled with doubt and text messages left to read. First dates that never made it the second, leaving me wondering what went wrong. Many times, it ended in disappointment.

A few weeks went by, and we headed to Miami to a large church to check out one of their services. We went down early and scooted around the city on electric scooters. After a fun day in the city, we got stuck in some wild traffic—hours and hours of sitting in the same place on the road. I would look over at him and feel like this couldn't be real. I enjoyed the traffic because it left us with a few hours to talk, and naturally for me, I like to not live in gray areas. So, of course, the words spilled out of my mouth.

"So...what is this?" I so badly wanted to know what he was thinking and feeling.

He replied, "Whatever this is, I want to pursue it."

I died on the inside. I felt like my soul left my body. Here I was in the car with the cutest man I had ever seen. He was cute, shy, funny, and a blast to be around. He was a gifted communicator and had a heart for people. I rested in knowing that whatever this could be, it would be really good. There was a joy in my heart and a pep in my step that I had never had before.

On our next date, we headed to an old arcade. It was filled with all of my favorite games—air hockey, Skeeball, and Pacman. We played games, laughed, and grabbed tacos for dinner afterward. The sun started to set, so we went to the beach until the dark of the night was upon us. We sat watching the reflection of the moon while the breeze blew my blonde hair in the wind. We laughed as we talked about what people were saying to us and how they inquired about our relationship status.

I asked him, "What do you tell people this is?"

With a little smirk, he looked at me and replied, "I wouldn't mind going to church tomorrow and telling them you're my girlfriend." I shouted YES. So, it became official. I was his girlfriend.

The morning came, and I picked out a black dress with periwinkle flowers to wear. He picked me up and we got some coffee as we headed to church. I was so nervous about what this would be like. His role was very prominent in the church, and that can be overwhelming at times. This church gave us an amazing community and so many friends.

I loved this season of dating. I got to listen to him teach and preach. These were and still are my favorite memories of living in Florida. The way that he led was inspiring—how he accepted people, and the way that they challenged me in my own faith.

Out of nowhere, Austin told me that his parents were flying in the following week. I thought that it was odd that they would come in out of the blue. Sure enough, his parents flew in, and right away that morning, Austin and I were going to go to the sunrise. Ten minutes before he got to my house, he told me that his parents hopped in the car and they were coming too. His dad was the first to get out of the car, and he gave me the biggest hug, followed by his mom and sister. We watched the sunrise, and I went to work.

After work, his dad called me an Uber and I met them for a late breakfast. We spent all of our meals with them and some time at the pool. It was so sweet spending time with them. We were only a month into dating at that point, but we spent nearly every day together. We went back to my house before dinner with his parents, and I told Austin, "I have loved spending every day with you."

And to my surprise he responded, "I wouldn't mind spending every day for the rest of my life with you."

I melted when we both looked at each other. At that moment, we both knew that we had met the one who we would do life with. That was the moment that affirmed why the Lord led me on this crazy journey. This is what I held on for. Austin was the reason I stayed.

That next morning, I went to the beach with his sister, and she told me why they came to Florida. The real reason why they booked a last-minute flight was because as soon as his parents heard how seriously he was talking about our relationship, they knew that they needed to come quickly. He met his dad for coffee and talked about his future with me. I wasn't sure what the rest of the year would look like, but I was eagerly excited for it.

As I reflected in this season, I couldn't help but see God. Austin pursued me like we were destined for each other from the beginning. And then there was his last name, Bouquet. I felt like God spelled it out for me so that I wouldn't miss the sign. That summer went by quickly as the talk of marriage was on the tips of our tongues. We went through prep for marriage and took a trip home to Minnesota. During my layover, I wrote this:

> *8/19/2019 Dallas Fort Worth Airport*
>
> *"What a day. I'm currently at the end of my nine-hour layover. I can't wait to get home. My heart is full. As I sit here at 31E waiting for my flight, I'm reminded of the last time I flew home in December. I was still fighting so much fear and stress with my stalking situation. No*

part of me really wanted to go back to Florida. I waited and waited for the year to end so that I could go back home to comfort. I'm so thankful I had the hard "yes" to stay in South Florida, believing that God wasn't done yet. To my surprise, he was quick in his timing, crossing Austin's and my path two weeks after I made the decision to stay. After all our conversations, I knew a proposal was in the near future and a wedding to soon plan. I'm completely blown away. God is so so so good. His ways are higher and so much better than mine. I'm so excited and praying with expectancy for all that's to come. It was so sweet—Austin sent me money for a coffee with a sweet little note. I am so blessed to be dating him! Tomorrow, I go dress shopping, and I just know that I'm walking out with a dress tomorrow. I just know it. I completely trust God with this season of life. As I lay on the hard airport seating, wrapped up like a pretzel, totally uncomfortable, I still found myself falling into a deep sleep. I've been in an uncomfortable season of life. Nevertheless, even here in the discomfort, I still am able to do all things that I would do comfortably. I just need to close my eyes, trusting the one going before me. Trusting the process, timing, and perfect will of my Heavenly Father. Lord, have your way!

This has by far been the most incredible year of my life. God, I see you. I see you so clearly. I see you in all things. All the Glory goes to you. You're so faithful, so loving, so kind, so near, so present. I trust you. I want to walk in the fullness of all that you have for me. I surrender. Lord, have your way. Open my eyes, oh Lord, open my heart. Jesus, use my life any way you need. I surrender. Have your way.

   KP

Austin flew to Minneapolis a few days after I got there. I was very nervous as I waited just beyond the baggage claim. There was something about bringing a boy home that made me giddy. But he wasn't just a boy. This was a man I knew I wanted to marry.

  I enjoyed showing him where I was from and introducing him to my family and all the things that make Minnesota home: the many lakes that we're known for, the quaint shops along the river in Anoka, and the best malt shop found all the way up on the North Shore, and just about everything in between. While I was home, I ended up buying a wedding dress and took it back to Florida with me. It was a weird feeling, holding my wedding dress in hand as I boarded my flight, not even officially being engaged yet.

* * *

A few weeks went by, and it was September. There are a few girls that would get together in the morning once a week and go to the sunrise. We'd all get together and sleep in my little 800 sq. ft one bedroom mother-in-law suite to have fellowship and spa parties before getting up really early. This week was no different than the other ones. We had facials with these weird self-heating face masks and painted our nails and stayed up way too late. I was kinda restless, waking up a few times before we had to get up, and I went back to bed with the intention of not going to sunrise as we have done before. This morning was different. I woke up from the nervous yell of one of my friends, and when I turned over, I would never forget the emotions she was displaying as she handed me a hand-written note. My heart was racing, and I had a pit in my stomach.

The note said:

Krysta,

I hope I was able to catch you by surprise.
I've been looking forward to this day for
months. It has been at the tip of my tongue and
always on my mind. Krysta, I knew within the
first date that you were special and within two
weeks I was going to marry you. I love you with
all my heart. I've loved every minute I've spent
with you and look forward to every next time

*I get to see you. I can't even tell you how much
I love you, so I plan on spending every day for
the rest of my life showing you... See you at
the beach.*
   -Austin

I was an absolute wreck trying to get dressed and ready knowing that he was proposing. I had the outfit that I picked out for this special moment. The girls and I were squealing and trying to get me ready as fast as we could. We drove with the windows down and music playing. I was doing everything I could to keep my heart rate down and not throw up from the nerves.

When we pulled up to the beach, I saw my sweet boyfriend waiting for me near the steps that lead down to the beach. I greeted him with a hug, and we walked with our hands holding one another. I saw the morning sun coming up over the horizon and the sweetest little candles, but my only focus was on him. His hands were warm and clammy, and his voice a little unstable when he spoke. We went over to the candles, and he got down on one knee. I don't remember much besides these words: "I know that the first part of your life was hard, but I promise to spend the rest of my life making the second half the best."

We soaked in those moments on the beach together, and our friends cheered and celebrated us. The ring he gave me was absolutely beautiful—a round brilliant cut diamond on a gorgeous rose gold band with six additional diamonds on the side. Two of the added diamonds came from his dad's mom and two came from his mom's mom. Austin selected two more diamonds to add on each side of those for a perfect little cluster of three. I thought it was so sweet—all the time and details that went into this custom ring that he designed himself were absolutely perfect.

After the engagement, we went to breakfast before I had to go to work. We spent those next few weeks and months planning our special day. I didn't want a big wedding or really one at all; I would have been happy to elope. With that in mind, we decided to get married that December and only have a three-month engagement. I was ready to be his wife.

Our friends threw us the sweetest engagement party and gave me a bridal shower. It was so sweet to celebrate over those three months. All of our friends and family rallied around us with so much wisdom and guidance.

That time flew by, and finally, it was December 14th and we were getting ready to say I do. This day for me came with many mixed emotions. It was hard missing my dad in these moments. I woke up that morning emotional and just wanted to be alone. I started off the day by having breakfast with two of my spiritual momma's at my favorite oceanfront restaurant. I sipped my hot coffee as I tried to take in every moment. They dropped me off at home and soon after my dear friend and bridesmaid picked me up.

We went to the local farmer's market and walked around a little bit and headed over to a friend of Austin's that hosted the morning. We enjoyed breakfast and I got in the makeup artist's chair to get ready. I didn't feel beautiful. I honestly thought I looked like a clown with how much makeup I had on, trying to cover up my acne. I pulled it together and got a few getting ready pictures with the girls. I love each one of them dearly, but it was a rough morning for me. I wasn't myself. I finished getting ready with all my bridesmaids and that morning flew by.

We took pictures along the ocean and the historic Worth Avenue that I would spend many of my days working at the little flower shop.

Soon, I was waiting to meet my groom at the end of the altar. I decided to walk myself down the aisle, even though I had father figures that would. It had been me and the Lord, so it would be me and the Lord taking this step into my new life of marriage.

My music didn't play, but I started walking anyway. And I walked FAST. There was no time for tears or another minute to pass. I was ready to marry this man.

The venue was an old warehouse converted into a surf museum a few miles from the beach. It was in a little warehouse district with small shops nearby. I wanted a blank canvas to work with, and this place had never done a wedding before. It had big industrial windows that I loved so much. We carefully strung Edison bulbs from the ceiling, and I made a beautiful hanging floral installation over the ceremony spot. Our decor was tasteful but simple—tropical greens lined the table, and the bridesmaids held delicate dried floral bouquets. As the night came upon us, our wedding looked like it was an old Florida wedding. With the amber glow of the lights and the surfboards that hung around us, I was reminded of how much I loved this place I now called home.

We snuck away to the ocean to get the first few photos of husband and wife. Husband and Wife. Those two words were always on my mind and so eagerly wanted. To me, they represented a man who would love me unconditionally and would support me and care for me. And now, I was a Bouquet...a freaking Bouquet. From designing flowers at four-teen, I never thought in a million years I'd have such a complementary last name. God was and has been woven in all the details. To me, it was a little wink—an "I got you covered." He loves his children, and I felt his love pour out.

We spent time with each of those that cham-pioned me along the way. It was beautiful to look around that room and see so much love in one place. So many of my friends and church family flew in from out of town. We ended the night early to catch our early morning flight to our honeymoon in NYC. I was living in the moments that I waited and prayed for.

I learned a lot this season. I learned that if the Lord is speaking to listen and not let go despite what

I see or feel. I was two weeks away from missing out on this because of how I felt. I'm forever grateful for those in my life who continue to push me past my comfort zone.

PART III
Hope Overflowing

CHAPTER 18

BECOMING HONEST

There have been so many times that the enemy has tried to tell me that I'm not healed or that I haven't found freedom from my past. There are days where there's a false sense of bondage when I have already been set free from it. Healing never stops. You don't just arrive at a place this side of Heaven where you're fully healed. It's not possible here. But if I'm honest, there are days that I've woken up physically different, feeling the weight lifted and joy restored. There were glimpses in the middle of my deepest heartache that God was still moving. I prayed that I'd have the eyes to see him move. I prayed for divine appointments.

Over the years, there were so many moments that I saw the hand of God on and at work in my life. Simple conversations held over coffee, spring flowers, prayers, books, and people passing through a busy city. Feeling hopeless and hopeful in a matter of minutes. Deep pain and joy in one breath. An understanding that despite what I see, there is still a joy for the things unseen. What's to come, I wait for with great anticipation. Healing feels like you're about to fall apart but knowing it's not your strength keeping yourself together. Healing is glued together with learning to give and receiving grace.

Life after grief looks different for me. It was a long drive through the wildlife refuge, a large iced americano "love rocket" with three shots and a splash of half and half two to three times a day. I'd always run into familiar faces at the local coffee shop, and this always brightened my day. It looked like sunsets and lemon bar ice cream. It was many trips to Minneapolis to just feel closer to my dad. It was many years of struggling and not understanding this in-between space. I had hope, but I was also growing weary. Many church services where I knew I wasn't standing in my own strength, for if I was my own, I wouldn't be standing. Moments where I felt the presence of God so strongly and had peace washing over me. I was grieving the loss of a parent who was never there and now never will be.

It's such a unique process to be a believer in Jesus, knowing a loved one was saved and has eternal life now with Jesus. You miss them dearly but rejoice knowing where they are is far greater than being where you are. In this, I found comfort.

I have learned that the enemy will do whatever he can to get you to believe that you're not healed, even after years of being on the other side of what you've been healed from. He does not want you to be free. This freedom is only found through Jesus. You don't arrive at a place fully healed nor is it possible to stay at a place as such. Healing is a process that never stops. It may go smoothly for years, until something triggers that memory of the time a person made you feel a certain way, the loss of your loved one or a traumatic event you worked for years to heal from. Whatever your trigger is, it will get you to believe that you haven't healed, and maybe you haven't. But I guarantee that if you look back, you can see that things don't affect you the way that they used to, especially if you're a believer. God continues to move us from hopeless to hopeful, from dark to light.

I still have days and weeks that I struggle. As I write these words, if I'm honest, I'm in the middle of a struggle. Expressing these words on a page that many will see is as uncomfortable as it is healing. I aspire to be open and honest when I was taught to be quiet. As many years have passed, these too are triggers for me. I have given myself space and grace to heal. Some struggles are familiar, and many are new—I have just made room to freely process these things honestly with myself. I have battled anxiety and its physical effects that it has had on me. There are days that I look in the mirror and I don't recognize myself. I still have nights that I cry myself to sleep. Parts of me are still broken, but I've learned to embrace them. Many days, I long for a piece of Heaven. I pause and find a little bit of it each day. At sunrise, a warm cup of coffee in bed, a word from the Lord by reading his word, a hug from my sweet husband, or through the head on my black lab resting on my chest. All you need to do is open your eyes. God is there, and he's moving. He's waiting for you to let him in.

I found healing and will continue to find healing. There really is one way that leads to healing, and that is through Jesus.

CHAPTER 19

GAINING UNDERSTANDING

One might ask, how could a parent do this and be okay with a child to be raised in this way? Let me be transparent: they weren't. My father's addiction stemmed from his childhood. My brother's addiction devastated my dad. He never wanted my brother to follow in his footsteps. My brother's addiction was far worse than my dad's addiction was. My mom enabled them for many years as she battled her own demons. She left my dad many times to try to break free from the abuse. This cycle was toxic. It's leaving and going back to the comfort of the dysfunction, even if it cost her everything. She didn't want us to grow up like her, without a dad.

I have found understanding, grace and forgiveness for my parents. My heart's desire is to honor them while I share this story. Yes, they had choices to make, but so do I. The choice is to walk in bondage or to be free. I made the decision to walk in freedom from my past. This is a decision only I could make. I made the decision to give them grace. Because I was forgiven, I need to be forgiving.

Let me be very clear: forgiveness does not mean to go back to what was. With forgiveness comes healthy boundaries for myself and for others. It's not forgetting. Although I needed to let go of the anger, I truly can never forget.

I have had many conversations that I recall falling into the same pit—walking in unforgiveness with the same words coming out of my mouth: "I will never see or talk to them again." For years, there was a separation from my family. But Jesus heals and restores those places and things that are broken if we're willing to surrender them.

Over the years, I have experienced his healing and restoration. I have seen his handprint in the details, even the smallest desires. One time, I went into a cute little gift shop a town over from where I lived. While I was browsing the store, I saw a blue bracelet with a unique quote on it. The bracelet was a little more than I wanted to spend, and I knew that I didn't need it, even though I really wanted it. I was the only person in the store, so I took my time browsing and ended up leaving without the bracelet. A few weeks later on a Sunday morning, a lady walked across the church's sanctuary and handed me a gift.

She explained to me that she really felt like the Lord laid it on her heart to give me this. It was the very same bracelet that I wanted. I was blown away.

The Lord cares about the smallest desires of our heart. In seasons of my life, he made it so evident that he was with me—seasons where I needed it. It's hard, at times, from being in seasons where I see him moving and at work in the details, or others where I'm not seeing him move in these same ways. These seasons are very much like the one I'm in right now as I write this book, and these are the things that I remember:

It's a relationship, and he never changes. Each season should look different. While I'm growing and learning continuously, I now expect my walk with the Lord to look different. My prayer is that I would be different on the other side of each season.

Rest in what he last told you or put on your heart. My deepest desire is to walk in the fullness of what he has for me. And right now, I'm writing this book. I may not see what he's doing in this season, but one day I will.

We live in a generation that desires immediate gratification. I'm guilty of this.

Just because you prayed for something doesn't mean it's going to happen the way that you thought it would. He hears our prayers, but that doesn't mean he delivers the answers the way that we painted them in our heads. And that's for our own good.

My heart longed for him to move, and I believed that he would again and again. I think that's what has gotten me to where I am today. My prayer was and is that he would be glorified come hell or highwater. Despite what is happening around me, I would continue to seek him out and have a dependency on him. Through my weakness, he can lead those I encounter to experience him. Through my faith, others would come to know him.

My mom's dad left when she was little, and she only was able to have a call with him when she was eighteen before she lost contact with him again. Many years went by, and my mom met her stepsister. He ended up getting remarried and had another daughter. At this point, my mom had still never met him. A few years ago, her son tragically passed away, and she invited my mom to the funeral, giving her the ability to finally meet her dad after over forty years had gone by. She turned down the offer, but I decided to pick it up. I got in my car and headed to the cities. I walked into the church into a sea of people that I didn't know. I found my mom's stepsister and she walked me over to her dad—my grandfather. The look on his face was priceless when she explained to him who I was. He had no idea my mom had any children, let alone that she was even alive. I sat with him for a while and made some small talk and took a photo with him. I left that day feeling grateful to have the ability to take opportunities to tear down any bitterness.

This was the first and the only grandfather that I was able to meet, since my dad's dad passed away when he was little and neither grandma remarried. He ended up passing away a few years later, and my mom never met him. I still find it crazy at times that I did and now she never will. I was willing to say yes to the hard things in life. I have found that time and time again, those are the best decisions I've ever made.

CHAPTER 20

UNTOUCHED

Since my brother is six years older than me, it always was interesting when he'd throw house parties. My parents were the laid-back type. They wouldn't care what he'd do at the house; in fact, they preferred that he throw a party at home, rather than worry about where he was. Since he was the cool older brother, I always wanted to be out there with him.

I was still shy, wanting to hide from all the people in my bedroom but as I got older, I got a little braver. The people would be everywhere. In the house, out by the fire, or in our large, detached garage. I would wander out into the dark of the night only to get questioned about who I was and what I was doing. I'd often reply with, "What are you doing here? I live here." Most responses would be, "You're so cute, you must be his little sister." I wasn't thrilled to see all these drunk girls falling into bushes or wandering around in the dark.

My mom did have a bowl that she'd collect the keys in. I remember one occasion when a drunk guy was trying to convince me to go get the keys for him that were in the bowl, and I thought he was out of his mind. I was young but not stupid.

Most parties at that age were safe. It would be some beer pong and nothing more—well, that I know of. My brother was still in his skater phase and would let me roll around on the skateboard in the garage with all of his friends. There were a few that I had known for years that I wasn't afraid of. Once, as I was going back and forth on the board, I remember falling forward and the board went the opposite direction. A young man let out a cuss word as he took the board to the shin—the worst possible pain you could feel. I felt so embarrassed and did the walk of shame back to the house.

These nights I look back on were actually dangerous. I was so young at the time, spending time with drunk guys in the wee hours of the morning. I see over and over again that God never stopped watching out for me. Although at the time I thought it was fun, I can see how messed up it was. I'm grateful that this didn't influence me as I got older. Once I did start to go out to parties, I knew that lifestyle was easy to leave behind. It is understandable to see how kids who grow up in homes like I did fall into alcoholism—it's being introduced and normalized at such a young age. It doesn't make it okay, but it does help to see where the root of it comes from.

CHAPTER 21

SHE PERSISTED

I would like to say that after I got married that things slowed down and the craziness stopped, but it didn't. The traumatic events stopped, but not my willingness to lay down my wants and desires. We loved our church and Florida family, but there was a part of me that felt the Lord calling us to move up north. After talking to Austin, I was discouraged when he said, "We're never leaving Florida." As a newly married woman, I knew I needed to respect that, but that didn't mean that I stopped praying for his heart to change. This wasn't the first time I felt this nudge at my heart that the door was closing and a new one was opening. Two months into praying for Austin to change his heart, he randomly looked at me one day and said he thought we should move up north. I would like to say that I was shocked, but I wasn't. I knew that was what the Lord laid on my heart months ago. We were a few months into Covid before we packed our bags and headed up north with the very little amount of belongings we had in our tiny mother-in-law suite where we had been living.

Moving to Ohio was rather difficult in the middle of Covid.

Everything was shut down, including the church we knew we wanted to attend. Florida wasn't as strict as it was here. It made for a really lonely and difficult first year of marriage. We were grateful for the family being close and that both of us had found jobs.

Moving closer to his family was so healing for me. It was a lot of restoration from my childhood. Things that I desired for many years were finally coming to pass. Although Ohio was very different from Minnesota, I was grateful to be back north. I missed the seasons and the summers. I missed the chilling winters that provide much needed rest. I missed the leaves changing colors in the fall and the enjoyment of a warm cup of coffee on a cold morning.

✳ ✳ ✳

Austin's parents are simply the best. His dad has pastored his home church for the last forty years and his mom oversees a non-profit that helps support those in foster care. His brothers have been brothers that I've always desired to have, and his sister has been the best addition into my life. It's really cool to look back now on my childhood and see the way that God has now given me so many desires that I had then. I deeply desired a Godly family, and I got just that. His dad has been a great father figure in my life, taking me in and claiming me as his own. I'm his "favorite daughter-in-law," even though frankly, I'm the only one right now, but even after there's two more, I'm still going to claim that title. I enjoy weekends spent with his parents and mornings spent golfing with my father-in law. My mother-in-law and I enjoy getting together and doing "girl things," like shopping and enjoying coffee at the local coffee shop. These are the days that younger me dreamed of.

Since moving here, I have found myself in a few different jobs and still working with flowers in some sort of form. Over the years, floral has been something I've been able to fall back on in so many seasons. It's provided a steady income and a sense of security when it comes to moving—I have never been to a town that doesn't have a florist. The job security is something that I have rested in as a florist until this past year. Now with being in full-time ministry, I have felt that the Lord has slowly started taking my desire to work with flowers away. I do love it, but I don't feel the need to constantly be doing it.

Moving in the first year of marriage was anything but easy. The church that we wanted to go to wasn't meeting back in person for six months after we got there. It took a while, but over time, we were able to make friends and find community, and for that, we're grateful.

In each job I have had, there's been a common theme. I tend to give it everything I have until I am completely burnt out. I love running fast and hard, but I tend to get carried away. When I reflect on my childhood, it makes a lot of sense. I'm not used to resting because it wasn't something I was able to do. There was always something happening, and I have always needed to work really hard if I wanted to get out of my current situation.

Over the last year, I have really struggled with rest. I'm grateful for my husband because he's so good at making sure I know when I'm going too fast and saying "yes" to way too many things. But he never stops me; he gives me a little nudge but with grace and love. A few times, he's just grabbed my hand at the end of a long night and started walking out the door, and that's when I really know "it's time to go." But rest doesn't come naturally for me.

CHAPTER 22

HOLDING ONTO HOPE

I would love to take some time to fill you in on what my life looks like now. Most of you I'm sure think I should probably be in a mental hospital or that I'm extremely dysfunctional. Yes, the past twenty-four years of my life have been bizarre, but for some reason, by the grace of God, I've been able to keep my sanity.

Now that we have been living in Ohio for a few years, we've settled down and bought a home. We have a sweet little Goldador that we love dearly! This dog has been everything I needed and more. We got him when he was only seven weeks old. Austin wanted a black lab, and I wanted a golden retriever, so we met in the middle. I wanted a dog for so long that once he said we could get one, I found a litter that would be available the soonest...in Texas. I had a wedding that I was doing flowers for and it just so happened that the puppies were ready that same week only nine hours from where we would be. I somehow convinced my husband to say yes to this crazy adventure. Rhett has been the best addition to our family. He's grown into the sweetest and most snuggly dog. He has helped me so much in the past year when it comes to struggling with stress, writing, and at times, my anxiety.

I stopped drinking coffee, and to my surprise, my anxiety disappeared. Coffee has been something that I would enjoy every morning, and I would also always be my go-to for an afternoon pick me up. Going to my favorite coffee shops was something I would look forward to when I was back home in Minnesota. It almost became a part of who I was. But it's worth giving up. I was willing to give up whatever it took to get rid of my anxiety.

I'm now in full-time ministry and my husband is pursuing his passion in business.

I have flown home many times over the past few years and still stay in contact with my family. I still have boundaries but with love and grace. I allow some trips to be spent with family and some I take time away for myself to catch up with old friends. I still love and miss everything about my little hometown. It's weird to go back and see people who never left and really haven't changed. I can't imagine what my life would look like if I never left. I have changed so much since the day I piled all my belongings and myself into that truck to go to Florida. I left the old me in that driveway that day.

Austin and I have been enjoying all the time spent with family and relaxing on our patio in the summer. Some seasons have been really busy for me in ministry and others have been restful. Nothing earth shattering has happened in a while. Or at least, it hasn't felt that way. Living away from home has nearly made the chaos disappear. I wrestled with this at first. Living out of state made me unable to run to the distress. The overdoses, fights, illnesses—you name it, I couldn't be there for it. I'd just have to take the calls and give it to the Lord. It wasn't my burden to carry.

There are days I still get "those" calls. And in seasons, I've had to politely ask my family not to call me about the relapses unless it is life or death. It began to take a mental toll on me. I was getting upset and worked up for no reason. That's the "cycle" that I fought years to get out of, and I realized that I was quickly going back into it.

We love our church and our pastors so much. They speak truth and they speak it boldly. I have never heard a church that does this with so much grace and love. They have made us feel so welcomed and so loved. As soon as I left the floral industry, I was ready to put my floral knife down for good. I was willing to give it all up to go into ministry. Going into it, I knew that ministry is a jealous lover, so I have to be careful to balance that and my family.

My prayer is that in the years to come, I'll be able

to continue to walk in the way that the Lord has called me—day by day in step with him.

It's hard to wrap my head around the fact that I'm sharing this story with you. It was one that I never thought I'd share. It's something that for many years, I kept close to me. I was afraid, ashamed, and embarrassed. I felt like a complete mess. The Lord, perfect in his ways, came along and changed everything for me. Those things didn't take away from who I was but made me into exactly who God created me to be.

CHAPTER 23

HOPE HAS A NAME

Maybe you picked up this book because you had no idea this book talked about Jesus. If this is you, I'm so grateful that you did, and that means I did exactly what I set out to do. My heart behind this book was for a believer and an unbeliever to pick it up. I didn't mean to "fool" you; I wanted to give you an opportunity to be encouraged because most unbelievers like yourself will never walk through the doors of a church or even listen to an online sermon.

The purpose behind this book was to shed light on a story that, unfortunately, many people that I have met have experienced. Many of those people have not gotten out of their situations or don't know how to heal. Life after childhood trauma, addiction, and tragically losing a loved one are all very tough things to experience, and it can be challenging to learn how to live life again.

I am not an expert on any of these things, but I have experienced life change in a radical way. I couldn't keep these pages to myself. This story isn't just mine; it's something that so many people can relate to, and I'd do anything to help a brother or a sister find freedom. I hope this book has opened your eyes to the reality that the real enemy doesn't even want this book in your hands. He doesn't want you to find freedom. He wants you to stay bound in this ugly cycle that you have found yourself in.

I found freedom when I laid my life down. When I surrendered everything that I had. I knew that I couldn't do any of this on my own. The seeds that were planted in my heart during Release Time when I was in third grade were still planted in me. When the local church watered those seeds, I was able to see things so much clearer. Yes, I know that many people may have never heard the message of Jesus Christ, maybe this is your first time, and you think I'm just a nutty writer because you have no idea what I was saying in most of this book. Today very well could be the day that changes the rest of your life. I pray that is it. I wrote this book with you in mind. The lost, lonely, shame-filled, hopeless, broken, and the addict. The truth is that we all fall short of the glory of God, but nothing is worse than falling short and not even knowing God.

I'm not here to save you, only Jesus can do that. I hope you can reflect on this story and have your eyes open to something you have never seen before. Hope has a name; his name is Jesus.

CHAPTER 24

WELCOME HOME

As you wrapped up that last chapter, I hope that it has gotten you thinking. I was born into a family of non-believers and had been lucky enough to get into the room with believers. I don't believe it was an accident that I have ended up here. The Lord, good in all of his ways, relentlessly pursued me. And he pursues you. The best thing I ever did was get on my knees and accept Jesus into my heart. That was the turning point in my life.

I have a little something for you.

I want to invite you to pray this prayer when you want to accept Jesus Christ as your Lord and Savior. If you read this book and you want to experience that life change, hope, peace, and strength that I have been able to experience, this is your chance. I can't guarantee that it will be anything like my story, but what

I do know is that your life will never look the same. I would like you to pray this prayer out loud:

> *Jesus,*
>
> *"Forgive me of my sins, Lord I believed that you died on the cross for me and was raised to life again. I confess with my mouth and believe in my heart that you are my Lord and Savior. Fill me with your Holy Spirit. I will live the rest of my life following you the best that I know how. Lord, I surrender my life and I give it all to you. My life is in your hands, Lord, help me to trust you."*
>
> *In Jesus' name*
>
> > *Amen*

If you prayed that prayer, WELCOME TO THE FAMILY! I am so excited for what God is going to do in and through your life. This is by far the most important decision you'll ever make.

If you got to this point and you're not ready to take this step, please don't put this book down yet. This story isn't over. You are still loved and cared for. I pray that this book will nudge you into processing your beliefs, and I know the Lord will continue to relentlessly pursue you. So don't be surprised if you think about this book long after you're done reading it. Let this be a reminder of the faithfulness of God!

CHAPTER 25

THE OTHER SIDE

Maybe you're reading this book and relating to the victim or the survivor of gang violence. Maybe you're the biker or the abusive father. No matter who you are, I want you to know that you're loved. You are seen. There is a place for you here on this Earth when you feel like you have gone so far in the wrong direction. When your kids don't want anything to do with you, I want you to know I was once one of those kids. The best thing my parents ever did was to step into a relationship with Jesus—they did this AFTER everything. I found forgiveness and grace for them, and I'm believing that for you, too.

I can't promise that every child who has turned a cold shoulder to you will come back into a relationship with you, but I do know this: My dad prayed every day and lit a candle for me for three years, and I had no idea. The Lord did a tremendous amount of work in my life. I would have never been able to forgive my father on my own and in my own strength. It was truly the Lord.

I want this to be an encouragement to you, pray. Pray harder and more intentionally than you have ever prayed for your children. Pray for divine appointments, people to have encounters will them that will point them to Jesus and soften their hearts. Pray that they would find a church and Godly community, Godly spouses. All of these things are so important and are worth praying about.

Maybe you were reading this book and you have or are currently struggling with addiction. I want you to know that you're not a failure, you are a child of God. You are seen and loved by your Heavenly Father, and you are loved by his bride—the church. It's the best hospital for the broken, and if you haven't checked one out yet, you should. I have seen the lives of so many addicts find freedom in those four walls. It is not a pretty building working these miracles. It is the son of God. Jesus has transformed so many lives of those wrestling the never-ending cycle of addiction. My heart goes out to you. I have prayed for you. Your family loves you more than you could ever imagine, even if they don't show it.

"I pray right now in the mighty name of Jesus that those chains that bound you would be broken, that the mental battle that you have been fighting would cease. I pray right now that your mind would be filled with holy thoughts, and I pray for peace where there wasn't any. I pray that Jesus would fill any cravings and desires that you so badly want again. I pray for strength that only comes from him to surround you. I pray that on this side of Heaven that you and your family would see you freed from your addiction."

Or, maybe it doesn't have anything to do with my story, and you're wrestling with the thoughts of the wrongs you have committed against someone. There is forgiveness for that. When you step into a relationship with Jesus, the old is gone. The greatest thing that you can do is pray for them and ask for forgiveness; Jesus will give you the peace you need.

You could be reading this as the enabling parent. I wrestled for years trying to understand why my mom made all the decisions that she made to enable my dad and brother. When it came down to it, she loved him so much she didn't want to lose him.

Having a child wrapped in addiction is a pain I cannot even pretend to comprehend. But I do know what it's like to have a parent and a brother wrapped in this mess. You love them so much that you'd rather watch them die in your house than on the streets. You have to make that decision for yourself if you're going to enable them or help save them. There are incredible programs to help those who want to get help. Enabling an addict only caused my mom to miss out on the majority of her thirties and forties.

Truthfully, she missed out on my life and my sister's life. She had to choose who she was going to take care of—her fifteen-year-old daughters or her twenty-one-year-old son. As hard as it was, I was grateful that she chose him and has worked hard over the years at not enabling him, finding help for him and standing up for herself. She deserves to live again—to no longer live in fear but to enjoy the rest of her life.

As you have read up to this part of the book, I'm so sorry if my story triggered something from your childhood. I pray that if it did, that you'd take the time to continue healing in that area. I know for many, trauma comes from childhood abuse. My father was abused as a child, and it carried over into how he raised us. Maybe that's what you're wrapped in. I want you to know that coming from a child that was verbally abused, I found forgiveness for my dad BEFORE he died. I have seen so many cases of people who came from abused homes that have created abusive homes. I know that my dad never meant to hurt us. His words cut deeper than I could have ever imagined. Did you know that the enemy uses those nasty words that came out of your mouth? He does and has done a great job with the next generation when it comes to fatherlessness. He has these kids fooled that fathers aren't loving and aren't present. It's exactly how he wants them to view their Heavenly Father. If he can screw with the relationship with their earthly father, he can really change the way you think about a father all together.

I know that it's not always dads who are abusive. But my prayer is that you would find yourself stopping the cycle. Acknowledge and apologize as soon as you can. Dads: own it and don't deflect it. Never blame your kids for your own lack of self-control. Be mindful that your place in the family is something that the enemy will do whatever it takes to destroy. You're the head of the house, the spiritual leader. Be mindful and watchful. Keep your eyes on your wife—fight for her and your marriage. Your kids are watching you. Don't be nasty with your words unless you want your kids to be nasty with their words. If you want your kids to have a relationship with Jesus, you better stop just dropping them off at youth group and park your car to join the Bible study happening down the hall on Wednesday nights. They need you to show up more than they need anything else. I have seen kids bring their parents to Christ. Parents, please lead the next generation this way; please don't leave it to anyone else. It's time to lead the next generation from our kitchens and living rooms. From the morning when they wake up until they go to school is sacred time. They are preparing to go into a battle that is unlike what we have ever seen, especially today. The school is slipping into a perverted, skewed worldly view trying to shape our children.

CHAPTER 26

LASTING IMPACT

If you are reading this book and think this book doesn't apply to you, I want you to see it from a different angle. It does. If you're reading this and you have been spared from walking through this kind of life shaking and traumatizing, I am thankful! I want to encourage you to:

1. Be a loving and caring family member or friend to someone that has or is walking through a difficult time.
2. If you're able, open your home to a foster child.
3. Speak up for those who can't speak for themselves.

I'm grateful for the friends in high school that loved me when I didn't know how to love myself. They cared for me and stayed up all hours of the night letting me cry and vent all my emotions.

I can't thank those families enough who opened their doors for me. The kids who shared with me when I came into their homes. They put my comfort above theirs.

So many people spoke up for me when they saw that things at home were not okay. I had people who believed in me and knew that I wasn't just a child crying wolf. I couldn't imagine where I'd be if not for those voices in my life.

CHAPTER 27

IT'S TIME

All in all, God has been at the center of my life and of my story. There isn't a place that I look and I don't see him. He was with me the night we were taken from our home, and he was holding me the nights that I cried myself to sleep. He knew what he had for me. He knew what was on the other side of the darkness that consumed me. He had plans for me that my mind couldn't even think of. I didn't know that there could be life, real life, outside of dysfunction.

He spoke my name and called aloud for me. Relentlessly, he pursued me. Surrounded by a body of believers, I saw the chains fall off of me. Abuse, insecurity, fear, depression, and shame no longer could call my name. The Lord wrapped me in his loving arms, and for the first time in my life, I experienced what the love of a Father should feel like. No earthly father can even come close to his love.

I have been blessed to sleep each night with peace. I no longer am afraid of what tomorrow will look like; he is already going before me. How beautiful it is to rest with such assurance! My faith has carried me farther than I ever could have imagined. Although I am a quiet and reserved person, I made a promise to God that if someone asks me to share my story, I will never turn it down because of my fear of public speaking. More times than I like to admit, I have gone in front of rooms full of people to share the faithfulness of God in my life. I have been in large churches and small churches. Conservative and Pentecostal. I even shared my story at an overnight sleepover at a church full of third-grade girls. Let me tell you that it was very hard to even find a part of my story that was appropriate to share with third grade girls. I shared the part of my story where I lived with different families and not my parents. At the end of the horribly spoken message, I had one girl come up to me that was in foster care. She could relate to me, and I got to pray with her. The Lord didn't need me to speak with eloquent words. He just asked me to speak.

And that's where I have lived for the last several years. I have a horrible fear of public speaking, but I have never said no. This story isn't my own and isn't mine to hold close. It's not for me that I'm sharing this.

In January of 2022, my church started the twenty-one days of prayer and fasting. This isn't one of those dieting fastings; this fast is something that as a Christian, is a time set apart to rid yourself of things that you desire to focus on your relationship with Christ. It's emptying yourself, ridding yourself of the things of this world. Many people will fast TV or phones. Our pastor encouraged us to actually give up something that would push us outside our comfort zone—something that would actually hurt. I decided to do a liquid fast consisting of juice to start and eventually incorporated beans, rice, and some soup. During this fast, I wasn't praying for anything specifically but for him to move in my heart—open my eyes and give me ears to hear. We were at least a week or so into the fast, and I turned on our bathroom light and looked into the mirror. "It's time," the Lord laid in my heart as tears welled up in my eyes. I knew at that moment, this book was what he was nudging at. I knew since I was in high school that I wanted to share this story in the form of a book. I never expected it to be now. I will never forget that feeling I felt in the bathroom. It was one of those moments that I knew that God was up to something. I didn't tell anyone, not even my husband. I prayed, "Lord if this is what you have for me, then open the door for it."

Three days later, I was meeting with a friend of mine for tea. She is the sweetest friend, and I love her dearly. A month earlier, I met her for coffee, and she told me about her grandson who was struggling with addiction. I could relate in so many ways and was praying for them. A few weeks later, I got the call that he passed away from a drug overdose. It hurt my heart to know the pain that her family was going through. After some time went by, I wanted to meet her again for coffee to just give her a big hug. We got to processing what had happened this past month and she stopped and said, "Your story prepared me for what I just walked through; I feel like the Lord used your story." Tears started to well in my eyes again. How great is our God? I was just sharing my heart with her because I know how hard that is. How crazy is it that I had the opportunity to share my story and it helped her navigate a situation she had no idea was coming? Only God.

But it gets better. She looked up and said, "Krysta, I think you need to write a book and this needs to be a movie." Tears were now streaming down my face, and I couldn't even fathom what was coming out of her mouth. "You have no idea what he laid on my heart three days ago," I replied. I cried and cried a little more as I shared what the Lord was doing in my heart.

I wrestled with what people might think or what my husband would say. At this point, he had no idea I wanted to write a book. I was honestly afraid to tell him because of how busy I was at work, and even though the Lord told me and confirmed it, I hadn't seen the door open yet.

A few more weeks went by, and I saw that my high school English teacher posted about someone publishing a book. I was curious, so I clicked on her page only to find out that she has had her own publishing company for the last several years. I quickly messaged her and scheduled a call. It was so sweet to talk to her and actually have her know parts of my story. And that's where I am now. She has been the sweetest to work with and has made this process a breeze.

The Lord spoke, confirmed and opened the door for this story. I pray that it inspires you and encourages you. Perhaps its time for you to share your story, maybe "its time" for you too.

CHAPTER 28

ONE OF THEM

Minnesota has been the sweetest place to grow up. As I've gotten older, I have fallen in love with everything that it has to offer. From the shops along the River in Anoka to the Ice cream shops on the North Shore. I love home. This may take many readers by surprise. Even though my childhood was awful, I still fly home three to four times a year. Minnesota is one of my favorite places to visit. But meeting a fellow Minnesotan is one of the things that make me so giddy. There's just something special about where I'm from.

The majority of my love does come from the church. The church is what makes me come back. I know I found a good church when I left four years ago and when I come home, they love me and act like I never left. It's a family. A bond. A grace filled relationship. They raised me up and they sent me out. They loved me more than I could have ever imagined and displayed Christ's love to me. I look forward to every trip home. I get a tea at the local coffee shop, often just hanging out there. It's my favorite place to see all my friends as they pass through on their morning route to work or afternoon workout. I just love these people. I will forever be "one of them."

I also fell in love with the little Bible store in our town. They have the cutest decor and gifts. I found myself there many times over the years. I would often get rings with little verses or words on them. I went through a phase where I would wear multiple rings on my finger, and I ended up giving so many away and then I'd go get more. It became a little ministry for me. If one would fit a girl that I was ministering to, I would let her have it. It was just a little thing that many people wouldn't pass up. These are the days I love and will forever remember.

I loved the summer nights spent on Mille Lacs, fishing and watching the sun go down. Nothing beats Minnesota summers. It's the warming up to the Great Minnesota get-together: The State Fair. The state fair's name doesn't lie. It's the best thing the state has to offer. I would go as a little girl with my dad. We'd conquer the big slide, stand in line forever for the milk and cookies, and would stay the butterfly tent as long as he'd let us. One year, we even got wacky hair done and a wax mold of our hands. We'd often stick around for the concerts. The last time I went with my dad we sat outside the fence and listened for as long as I could remember, singing out our favorite songs together. These were happier days in my childhood.

Minnesota summers ended by meeting the sweet season of football camps. I never played sports throughout school, even though I really wanted to. My family was never able to afford the fees for us to play. So, I did the second best thing—I managed. I managed football, basketball, baseball, and soccer, and I competed in FFA. I never felt like I was missing out. I loved spending time with all the guys; they really did take me in as one of their own. A lot of them became great friends over the years, I guess it was different because I had no motive with them. I kept to myself and took my job seriously—except when it came to videotaping the football games for them to watch film. I didn't have the steadiest hand and definitely didn't pay enough attention to where the ball was going. It was fun to be with them season after season. Running water out on the big football fields under the Friday night lights was a highlight of my high school career. The chilling fall nights spent with a bus of sweaty guys wasn't ideal, but it made me feel like I belonged to a team—a group of guys that respected me. A group of guys that showed me that not all men are "bad." I think I managed so many men's sports because I lacked positive relationships with men in my life. With my dad and brother being so absent, I longed to just have guy friends. I was still very shy and timid when I talked to boys, so at times, it was overwhelming.

High school had a lot of hard times but there were also many great memories. I competed with FFA in a floral competition and ended up making it to state. It was so fun to be able to compete in something that I was passionate about.

Being from Minnesota will always be something that brings so much joy to my life. I never thought I could love a place so much. I still get butterflies every time I go home. It brings me so much joy to be reminded just how far the Lord has carried me.

CHAPTER 29

GROWING THROUGH THE EMOTIONS

I want you to know that it's okay to go through the emotions of what you have walked through or what you're walking through right now. What I struggled with during and after my journey of finding freedom was the lack of emotions. I didn't give myself permission to grieve. I carried the weight of other people for so long that I became numb.

I was feeling so many emotions that weren't meant for a child to feel. For years, I wrestled with my emotions and found the freedom to feel them again. I shut down. I didn't want to make room to be hurt again, especially when it came to my dating life. I went out with a guy who lied repeatedly to me, and for some reason, that didn't turn me away. Lying was a given in my house growing up. I found that I would see myself slipping into being okay with a guy that had the same toxic traits that I tried to leave in the past. It was all too familiar. When he'd be dating someone else, I'd be nothing until they'd break up again. He'd be quick to text me the next time he needed a date; he knew I wouldn't say no. I was used to being left out or a second choice. I found myself tolerating the same dysfunction I fought so hard to get out of—it was no surprise that dysfunction was so attractive to me. It wasn't until my first year of college that something changed in me. I stopped answering the drunk calls and the empty texts. I found my worth.

I allowed myself to experience the fullness of what God had for me. When I started dating my husband, I felt peace like I had never felt before. I've now been able to experience the full emotions of life again.

My biggest guide is keeping my peace. If it's going to cause me to lose my peace, then it needs to go. If not doing something will make me lose my peace, then I need to do it.

CHAPTER 30

HE'S NEAR

In every season, I feel like I have significantly changed. I'm learning to navigate what that looks like in this season. Some people hate change, but change isn't a bad thing. Without change, there is no growth.

While writing this book, I have felt reserved, sitting back and just reflecting. I've had seasons that I was more on fire for Jesus and seasons where I've been more loving, caring, and intentional. Days where I was more present. There were times in my life where I'd run to every broken home or hopeless situation—not to say that I wouldn't do the same right now, because I would.

I have received gut-wrenching phone calls about friends' loved ones who passed away. I got a call from one friend specifically when I was leaving church; her friend's family just got into a tragic accident, and one of the daughters passed away. This accident happened hours away up north. I picked her up and we headed up north. The family was still in the hospital, shaken up by everything they just experienced. We got to the hospital, and she went back to grieve with the family while I sat in the waiting room that overlooked Lake Superior.

After a while, she came out with some of the family, and we had the opportunity to love on them and I had a chance to pray with them. I barely knew one of the sons; I really didn't know the family. But I didn't feel out of place. The Lord placed me right where I needed to be. Anyone could have brought her up there, but the Lord knew that I had a willing heart. I didn't run away from messy people; I would run towards them.

Some time had gone by, and I was at work waitressing. I tried to stay off my phone when it was busy because there would be no time to check it until after my shift. My sister knew when I'd be working, so she would wait to call me until after work. It was a normal shift, and I was working in one of our busiest sections, when I heard the restaurant's phone ring. That was normal with how many calls we got for take-out and reservation questions. Except this time, the other server handed it to me, and on the other end of the phone was my sister. My heart sank because I knew she would only call me at work if something bad happened.

"Krysta, you need to leave right now. We need to get to Minneapolis. It's not good."

I ripped off my apron and ran out the back door after giving my tables to another server. I got in my car and drove as fast as I could to my sister. She proceeded to tell me that our next-door neighbor growing up, one of our best friends, got hurt at a party. After a few drinks, a kid that I had gone to high school with hit him on the head with a hammer twice. They rushed him to the hospital, but it wasn't looking good.

His family lived in Colorado now, so we were all that he had. The doctors told us that in the scan it showed that he was most likely not going to make it through the surgery. They told us to prepare for that. His mother and sister were on the next flight into Minneapolis when we headed down to the cities, and they were expected to arrive after the surgery.

I remember looking at my sister as she wrestled with the fact that we were told he wasn't going to make it. But I wasn't accepting that. I knew my God. I had seen his faithfulness over and over again. I believed wholeheartedly that my God was able to save him; I didn't think that God was done with him yet. There were so many non-believers looking into this hopeless situation. My heart longed for God to move, for a miracle. My heart was to see him be glorified through this. I was confident.

We arrived at the waiting room and waited for what felt like forever. We got the call, and the doctor told us that he miraculously made it through the surgery and would make a full recovery. Minutes after the call, his mother and sister arrived, and we greeted one another with a warm hug. They have been and will always be family to us.

They went back to see him in recovery, and he was in pain but was still his hilarious self. We all walked away grateful and with our hearts full.

I had peace knowing my God. I trusted him that if he did take his last breath, that it was his time to go. I was fully willing to accept that, but I struggled with not knowing if he knew Jesus. That same boy I prayed for a miracle for is now sober, a father to the sweetest little boy, and has accepted Jesus Christ as his Lord and savior. God wasn't done writing his story.

I have been to candle lit services for many students that we have lost in our community. I have wandered down school hallways to hug my teachers after losing a student. I helped hand out bracelets and stayed up countless nights to listen to someone grieve. I've received the drunken suicidal calls from friends.

I have gone out on a limb to reach out to a girl who tragically lost her boyfriend and I supported her for that season in her life. Whether it was getting our nails done, holding their hands in church, or just listening to them; it didn't matter what it was, I wanted to give back because of what I was given—more support than I could have ever imagined. When our community lost a young life, we all showed up even if we didn't know them. The church was always open and willing to be there. When the community lost someone, we all lost someone.

I have visited friends in rehab and in treatment centers to show as much of my love and support as I could. I have slept on friends' floors who were wrestling with suicidal thoughts to be sure that they made it to the sunrise. I had friends wrapped up in drug addiction, too many DWIs, parents going through divorces and having affairs. Girl friends with boy problems, and boy friends with girl problems. Unfaithful relationship after unfaithful relationships. Many of these friends of which I don't keep in contact with anymore. A handful of them I can still call in the middle of the night after years of not talking. One being someone I called this year to be with my sister when I couldn't be, and he did more than just that. He spent days with her to make sure she was okay. Those are the people that we all need in our life.

I've been to a friend's parent's funeral. Once, when I was in my first year of high school, a friend's mom passed away, and her dad wasn't in her life. She lived with her grandparents who only lived a few houses away from me. She asked me to be with her for the funeral and the viewing of her mom. I was horrified, but I couldn't imagine the pain she was feeling. Despite what I was wrestling with, I knew that no matter what I felt, I needed to be in the room with her.

Some of you may be reading this and thinking,

"Man, this girl really loves to talk about herself and what she's done for other people." But that's not the point in sharing this. I share this because I have seen Jesus in all of these places. Where the broken and hurting are—that's where I have seen him move in ways that I could have never imagined. It's in the mess and in the heartbreak that God meets us in the exact way that we need him. I'm just grateful he used my willing heart to give me a front row seat to what he was doing.

CHAPTER 31

OPENING UP

One of the hardest things that I had to walk through was opening up to people. At a young age, I was trained so strictly to lie and never tell anyone about what I went through or what I was going through.

It was lies that I told myself over and over enough to even confuse myself on what was true. I convinced myself that I was the problem. I was so convinced for years that nothing was wrong with them. It was a constant war in my head.

As I got older and started finding the courage to open up to my friends, teachers, and mentors, I remember how it made me feel. I would start to sweat, my hands would get fidgety, and I would have to fight to get the words out of my mouth. So many people would look at me in disbelief. "That sounds like something out of a movie," many would reply. I was afraid that my story would be so much that they wouldn't believe me. But each time I shared it, something shifted within me. I started to grow stronger. I started to heal.

I remember talking to guys that I was interested in, and it was terrifying to put my messy heart on the line. I was so afraid that someone wouldn't want anything to do with my broken, messy, and tired heart. I was grateful for those who didn't shy away from my brokenness. I'm grateful for the one who wanted to love this mess of a person for the rest of his life, but I'm also grateful for the ones that didn't work out. I wasn't even going to mention those in this story, but honestly, this story would look incredibly different without them. The guys that listened and walked with me through some of the darkest days of my life. The days after I lost my father. The days that I didn't want to help myself. They deserve the space to know that if they pick up this book, that their time wasn't wasted but it actually helped someone get to where they're going. It's not often that someone tells you that you helped them. I want to be a person who never misses the opportunity to thank those who, good or bad, helped me in my journey.

I remember meeting my husband. Not too long into knowing him, I shared my story. He listened so intently. He was patient with me, and my past didn't stop him from pursuing me. He didn't use it as leverage or prey on me like some guys tend to do when they see a broken girl. My husband loved me and gave me grace to walk out the God-given calling on my life. I needed someone to do life with, someone who believed in me enough to run alongside me. I'm grateful he listened to my story and chose me despite what I've walked through.

I am no longer afraid to tell my story. The reality is that it's God's story. He's written every page and is woven in the details. I made a promise to God that I will always share this story.

CHAPTER 32

YOUNGER ME

Every time I think about how much I've gone through; it makes me take a step back and pause. I couldn't imagine going through it now. I honestly can't believe the strength that I had to overcome these trials at such a young age, but it truly was the Lord. Most days, it feels like a different lifetime to me. Life looks so different now.

I'm proud of my younger self. She did what she set out to do, what she longed for. She fought for freedom, and she found it. She dreamed big dreams and she pursued them. She left her little hometown, left comforting relationships and the comfort of her community. She grew spiritually and emotionally. She learned to count it joy come trials and heartbreaks. Fear rarely stopped her. There are days that I miss younger me. She lived life on the edge. Her ministry was thriving, and she loved people so well. I often find myself more reserved in this season of life—could it be that I'm healing more now in this season writing this book than I have my whole childhood combined? I think so. Younger me didn't have time to process every emotion with the constant chaos. She thrived on it.

It was those numb and heart wrenching moments where I would meet Jesus. Those long dark nights—that's where he was. I experience him differently here. I'm not as desperate as I once was, and I wish I was at times. There was a dependency, a trust. I wholeheartedly believe that Jesus changed everything for me. He wiped every one of my wrongs clean. He has been and forever will be the perfect father that I desired. He saved me and set me free. This isn't religion; it's the most important relationship I have ever had.

I look back and I see a mess—a lost, and broken-hearted girl. She just wanted to be held, loved, and cared for. There is so much grace for her. She beat the odds. And more than that, she looked fear in the face and called it a liar. She declared truth over her life and took back what was hers. A life full of LIFE.

I'm not able to get my innocence back, and that's okay.

I have Jesus.
I don't have all the answers,
but I have Jesus,

and that's more than enough.

Today, I was reflecting on my age. I stopped, and I couldn't believe that I'm now twenty-four. Most people would say that is very young, but I often feel like I should still be eighteen or twenty. Have I really been removed from my childhood for ten years?

I often wonder what life would have looked like if I would have never left my hometown. I can't even imagine what it would be like. Some days, I feel like it would be quiet and peaceful to live in my small town. But looking back, I would not have seen God move in so many incredible ways. I wouldn't have my sweet husband or my Goldador. I've been a part of big churches and small churches, and I love them both.

I wrestle with wanting to forget about my childhood, but at the same time, I never want to forget the faithfulness of God in my life. I never want to forget what he has done for me. So, that's why I find myself writing this book; he's been too good to me to forget. Rather than forgetting, I'm sharing my story.

CHAPTER 33

HOME AGAIN

I left my little hometown's local grocery store with a dozen of lavender roses in the front seat of my car, and I reach for my phone to call my mom. This isn't something that I do often enough. She was happy to hear my voice on the other end of the call.

"Are you home?" I asked.

"Yes," she replied. "Remind me what day you're flying in."

I responded and she was shocked to hear that I was only two minutes away from her house.

I got the not so good butterflies in my stomach. I passed the bowling alley and the two driveways before I reached the cluster of mailboxes. I started to head down her long driveway, looking at every detail of the houses that lined the streets of my childhood. I turned left down the last part of the driveway past the no trespassing sign. I started to have a hard time seeing. My hands went numb, and I couldn't feel my feet. It was getting hard to breathe. I could feel the physical effects this place had on me.

I started verbally telling the fear to leave.

"Fear, you need to leave. Fear, you have no place here. Fear, you need to go. This isn't yours anymore."

As I got out of the car, I was still trying to get myself to snap out of it. I reminded myself to walk in the authority that every believer has access to. I had left that fear years ago, but fear didn't stop calling my name. I stepped one foot in front of the other without being able to feel anything. I got to the front door, and I start to get a grip.

My mom met me on the front step. A lot had changed. She was the thinnest I had ever seen her. But she was still my beautiful mom. Her heart has always been kind. Her condition, however, showed how much turmoil she has been through.

Our conversations were kept short and shallow. I didn't have many words to say. It was hard to recover from all the emotions I was facing. I wandered around the garage looking at objects from my childhood. So many things were still there right where I left them.

The house was a lot older and had collected many more items since I had last been there. The place was almost unrecognizable—it grieved me. This place was not a happy place. I still wrestle with memories that were created there.

Being home was hard—sickening, really. The whole twenty minutes was more than enough for me. It made every part of my body cringe. But there's victory there. The Lord delivered me from that fear many years ago. It no longer had a place in my childhood home anymore.

As hard as these memories can be to recall, my life happened here. When I came home from college for Christmas break, I remember the Lord telling me that my mom's heart was ready. I grabbed my Bible and got into my car. I went to her house and took her into my childhood bedroom. After a short conversation, I prayed the prayer of salvation with my mom and she accepted Jesus Christ as her savior. I will never forget what she said: "I can physically feel the weight lifted off of me. I've waited my whole life for this."

I went to sleep crying and woke up the next morning crying, too. Huge life shifts had happened here.

EPILOGUE

When you're reflecting on my story, I want you to remember these three things:

- Only I could make the decision to change the course of my life into adulthood.
- I was a victim, but I made a decision to not live like one.
- Only by my faith was I able to get out on the other side and to have hope in the thick of it.

If you find yourself in an abusive home, I'm praying for you. There is a safe feeling in familiarity, even when the familiar atmosphere isn't safe. It's not until you leave the dysfunction that you realize how bad it is. You don't want to go back, but at the same time, you don't know anything else. And your mind starts to wonder what might happen to you if you leave. Will they hurt themselves? Will they hurt who's still at home? Will they find me and hurt me? Disown me?

I believe in freedom for you. I want to encourage you that God is always there for you. He is with you when you wake up, and he's with you when the tears roll down your face as you lay down to sleep. When fear is paralyzing you, he's calling out to you. If I could personally come and pluck you out of your situation, I would. No one deserves to be where you are; no matter where you have been or what you've done—you don't deserve it. It took me years to speak up. I was afraid and I had no voice. I want to encourage you to first find Jesus and a local church. Make those people your community. I know speaking up is scary, but you need to. Even in small ways.

I remember the day that a cop looked me dead in the eyes and told me I needed to speak up. And I did. I remember the moment that I left and found freedom and the words that rattled me. "I thought that I would have to come to your house and put you in a body bag if you didn't leave." These chilling words came from a place of uncertainty. These words are why I left. I knew that's how I felt at times but it was different coming from someone else, let alone a police officer. I didn't know if I'd make it to some mornings. I can't even tell you how many prayers I have prayed that I have gone like this: "God, I promise if I live to see tomorrow I will...."

I got to a point that many of us in that situation have to get to. A point where you get a strength to stand for yourself and to make a decision to create a life far greater than you have experienced. I pray that this book can be an encouragement to you. That is it possible to walk through this. And more than just walk through it, but to get on the other side and look like nothing you did.

Something that I would do was pray for those who hurt me. I prayed for my parents and for my brother. I'm grateful to now to be able to see both my parents come to know Jesus since then. Pray for them. They need it. They don't mean to hurt you. They are just as bound as you are. But you are in control of the decisions you make, and so are they. It's no excuse. You don't deserve it. Your grades didn't cause this. Your personality or behavior didn't play a part in it. For years, I often thought just being alive caused my dad to use. No child deserves to feel that way.

Maybe it's an abusive partner. Many feel like that they can't get a divorce and they stay in the abusive marriage due to a biblical view point. Divorce isn't a sin. Sweetie, you're free to go if the Lord releases you. If you're being abused, you're free to go. Go start over. It's time to get up again. It's time to live and love again. You need to find yourself again. It may take time to find yourself, but you will. You don't deserve what they have said to you. You are not those words. You're unstable. You're scared. There's grace for staying longer than you should. The false hope that things will work out is a really difficult battle. I pray that you'll find a community that will love you and pour into you. I pray that you'll find freedom.

If you're the one wrestling with a family member battling addiction, I'm so sorry you're going through that. The late nights and endless tears are seen by God. The sick feeling in your stomach when your phone rings. The hospital and treatment visits. The numbness after a decade of getting the call that they have overdosed again. The money that you gave or the things that were stolen. The lies that you never thought they'd tell. The endless calls to find them. Checking on them in the middle of the night to see if they're breathing. I see you. I believe in freedom for you. I still to this day pray for freedom for my brother. And I'm believing for your family too. It's hard. But I have given it to the Lord. He loves him more than I ever could. My brother has to make the decision that he wants help and to live that out. I can't do that for him, as much as I wish that was the case.

If you read this book hoping for it to be a perfect guide to help you through your situation, I'm sorry to let you down. I don't have every answer for you of the perfect road map for the course of your life. I can't reiterate this enough—only by my faith in Jesus Christ was I able to trust the perfect plan for my life. He is the keeper of that map. He knows every mountain top and every valley that I have walked through, and he knows everyone that I will walk through it with.

I was a victim of verbal abuse. Words have hurt

me and made me feel like I wasn't enough. Although I walked through victimhood, I made the decision not to live like a victim. I could use it for every excuse that I may ever need, or I can own my actions and heal from it. I could stay laying on my couch living in the past, or I could create a life far greater than I could ever imagine. I picked the second option. Were there days that I would stay on the couch? Yes. But I didn't stay there very long. I knew that God didn't allow me to go through all of that turmoil to lay on the couch. I was missing the opportunity to be used by God. He is willing to use any of us that are available, if we just allow ourselves to be.

ACKNOWLEDGMENTS

I have seen the faithfulness of God. I have seen lives change, hearts of stone soften, and many come into relationship with Jesus. I have seen marriages get saved, demons flee, and chains fall off people's lives. I've seen miracles, powerful prayers, and the simplest of prayers come to fruition. I've seen broken families mended. I have seen people with no hope find hope. I have personally walked through dark valleys and still have hope in the living God.

I don't believe that we're called to live a life of comfort. He's called us to live outside of our comfort zone—trusting when we can't see, can't comprehend, and don't understand. He's called us to sit in the uncomfortable places that grow us immensely. As I sit in an uncomfortable season where the world would say it's okay to give up and give in, I find myself sitting at the feet of Jesus, waiting on him.

I want to thank those who have helped me get

this far in life. First, I need to show honor where honor is due—to my parents. It's been my prayer that this book would still share the truth and honor them. They did the best they could with what they were given, and so did I. I wouldn't change anything that happened. I am grateful for my story.

My mom has overcome so many difficult and unimaginable losses in her life, and she has managed to keep going. She has sacrificed a lot for us kids, and I'm thankful for that. She wears her heart for all to see. She's a person that you can always call and will have an open door. I love her so much.

My story wouldn't be what it is without my dad. He made us endure great trials, and I wouldn't change any of it. Each trial he allowed us to face was something that formed me into the woman I am today, and for that, I am thankful. I know that he loved each one of us so much. He was biker-tough but had the heart of a servant—my dad truly was a mix of them both. He had one of the hardest of hearts but came to know Jesus, and that changed me for the better. I miss his blue eyes and spontaneous adventures. Life has looked different since he left. My heart hurts in a way that I never thought it would hurt. I felt an emptiness that my Heavenly Father has continued to fill. Without my story, I don't think I would have the relationship that I have with the Lord today. My dad made me rely on my Heavenly Father, and because of that, I have been blessed beyond measure.

I want to thank my brother. I love him dearly and I pray that one day he will come to know the Lord. I am grateful for each day he's here on Earth. I pray often for healing from his addiction. I know it has taken a great deal of strength for him to still be here. I miss him and our relationship. I love him more than any words that I can write. I'm choosing to believe that he'll find freedom from his addiction on this side of Heaven.

I'm extremely grateful for my twin sister. God knew I couldn't come into this crazy life without her. I wouldn't have wanted to go through any of that alone. Her strength and beauty inspire me. Her generosity challenges me. Her laugh is contagious, and her presence is fierce. I couldn't imagine what life would look like without her; she compliments me in ways that only she can. There's a safety with her that I will never experience with anyone else. Nothing hurts like my belly when I'm with her, laughing so hard that I can't stop the tears from streaming down my face.

To my extended family that has stepped up when I needed it the most, especially when it came to practical things that a child needs. The early morning city view of the Minneapolis farmers' market to get artisan soap that sparked a love for local markets. The sleepovers and buttered toast that somehow tasted better than anywhere I've ever eaten it. The warm embrace of a hug after an emotional day. Your homes have always been a safe place for me to sleep.

I am forever grateful for those memories and for your loving embrace.

To the families that took me into their homes in different seasons of my life, I wouldn't be where I am if it wasn't for your open arms and caring nature. I lived with multiple friends, family, and members of my church. I vividly remember the tear-filled nights where I didn't want to go home ever again. The pain and the heartache were overwhelming but not enough to drown out the love that I was surrounded with. I love to reflect on those seasons because that's where I saw God at work the most in my life. When I return home a few times a year, it never fails to remind me of the impact that each of you have made on my life. I walk through the same doors of the church that I did as a young, scared girl. I see the same faces that never cease to greet me with such love and compassion. My small Minnesota town will always be home, and you'll always be family. Without the church being the church, my life would look so different.

The jobs that allowed me to fail but showed me grace, taught me consistency, and to leave my troubles at the door to be able to serve those right in front of me. Whether it was at the local breakfast restaurant or in the grocery floral department, I was positioned so perfectly to serve those in my community, despite my world crashing down all around me. You taught me how to strive for excellence in all I do and that my age doesn't decide what doors the Lord will open.

To my friends that became family: I'm grateful for you. Many friends have gone in different directions, but that doesn't take away from the impact they have had on my life. There are many of you that I wish I still had a relationship with. My life is better because of you; all the breakfast dates, lunches, and coffees. The weekends spent together and the endless sleepovers. I will always cherish those memories.

I'm grateful for my pastors that have helped guide me along the way. The church plays one of the biggest parts in my story. It was because the church was being the church that my life was forever changed. It's a story that I will never stop sharing. I'm thankful for each pastor and the impact they have made and continue to make in their communities. I'm blessed to have been mentored by so many incredible leaders.

Lastly, I want to thank my husband. He's been a true gift to me. My life has looked so different since he came along. He's given me a godly family that constantly encourages me. His love for the Lord is evident in all that he does. I can't thank him enough for allowing me to walk out my God-given calling. His drive encourages me and challenges me to do the best in all I do.

Austin,

Thank you for praying and believing in me when I come to you with a wild word that the Lord has given me. Writing this book is up there on one of the craziest things I have ever done. I'm so blessed to be your wife; I can't wait to see what the Lord is going to do as he continues to write our story.

I'm grateful that it was finally "time"
to share my story.

ALL GLORY BE TO GOD!

ABOUT THE AUTHOR

Born and raised in Princeton, Minnesota, Krysta Bouquet's childhood brought her face-to-face with the brokenness of this world. Now, living in Ohio and serving in full-time ministry, Krysta felt compelled to share her story.